Fly Fisherman's Primer

Other books by the authors:

The Basic Manual of Fly-Tying

Expert Fly-Tying

Flyfishing Tips, Techniques & Strategies of the Experts

Fly Fisherman's Primer

Paul N. Fling &
Donald L. Puterbaugh

Foreword by Gary LaFontaine

STERLING

New York / London
www.sterlingpublishing.com

Library of Congress Cataloging-in-Publication Data

Fling, Paul N.
  Fly fisherman's primer / Paul N. Fling & Donald L. Puterbaugh. — Rev. ed.
      p. cm.
  Includes index.
  ISBN-13: 978-1-4027-4535-5
  ISBN-10: 1-4027-4535-4
  1. Fly fishing. I. Puterbaugh, Donald L. II. Title.

  SH456.F55 2008
  799.12'4—dc22

                              2007035199

10 9 8 7 6 5 4 3 2 1

Published by Sterling Publishing Co., Inc.
387 Park Avenue South, New York, NY 10016
© 2008 by Paul N. Fling and Donald L. Puterbaugh
Distributed in Canada by Sterling Publishing
^{c}/o Canadian Manda Group, 165 Dufferin Street
Toronto, Ontario, Canada M6K 3H6
Distributed in the United Kingdom by GMC Distribution Services
Castle Place, 166 High Street, Lewes, East Sussex, England BN7 1XU
Distributed in Australia by Capricorn Link (Australia) Pty. Ltd.
P.O. Box 704, Windsor, NSW 2756, Australia

Book design and layout: Susan Fazekas

Printed in China

Sterling ISBN-13: 978-1-4027-4535-5
        ISBN-10: 1-4027-4535-4

For information about custom editions, special sales, or premium and
corporate purchases, please contact Sterling Special Sales
Department at 800-805-5489 or specialsales@sterlingpublishing.com.

IN FOND MEMORY OF

GARY LAFONTAINE, MENTOR

FOR AN ENTIRE GENERATION

OF FLY FISHERS.

Thanks to the manufacturers of
equipment for the use of the
photos of their equipment.

A special thanks to Kip Beech
for his photo work.

CONTENTS

FOREWORD TO THE FIRST EDITION

A few years back my friends Paul Fling and Don Puterbaugh asked me to provide a quote, a personal endorsement, for their book about basic fly-tying techniques. These blurbs for advertisements might seem harmless enough, but they should always be given carefully—a reviewer should never cheapen his name by touting a product he does not support fully. He should not do it for any reason, even friendship. So that first book, *The Basic Manual of Fly-Tying* (Sterling Publishing Co., 1981), would have to earn whatever praise it received from me.

Two readings of that book left me no closer to a decision. Part of the problem was that it had been so long since my own beginnings as a fly-tyer that I was unable to judge the effectiveness of the book as a teaching tool. It was written in a concise, clear style, and it contained extensive illustrations. But was that enough? Was there anything about *The Basic Manual of Fly-Tying*—which at first seemed almost too straightforward—to merit its addition to the already extensive literature on the subject?

The easiest way for me to solve the dilemma was to conduct a test with a beginning fly-tying class. Students, divided into four large groups, were each given a different book before their first meeting and were told to come back prepared to tie a fly. The results were startlingly clear: those who had read *The Basic Manual of Fly-Tying* significantly outperformed the others (even those who had used the classic *Fly-Tying* by Helen Shaw). Obviously there was something special about this unpretentious, instructional text. It received my unqualified endorsement.

Imagine for a moment how difficult it is to write and illustrate without pretension. And yet every time a writer or illustrator decides to show off for the reader, he makes it harder for the beginner to learn from the book. So few creative people can resist embellishing even a simple instruction with alternatives: Do such and such; unless, of course, the wind is brisk or the sun is low or the water, and then, in order of appearance, do this or that or this. Writers, especially, often refuse to present information simply. Why? Because they have a great fear of being considered simple.

Paul Fling and Don Puterbaugh are anything but simple. They distill their years of angling and teaching experience into their books. They understand the wonderful complexities of fly-fishing as well as anyone, but they are such good instructors on paper and in person that they naturally avoid confusing the beginning angler with such intricacies. With their good friend, Bob Damico, a multitalented man who acts not only as photographer but also as general adviser for their books, they produce texts that instruct rather than overwhelm their readers.

The beginning fly fisherman is going to enjoy thoroughly and, maybe more importantly, learn from the *Fly Fisherman's Primer*. The numerous illustrations, some of which show both top and side views of a stream, accentuate the main points. The writing makes this book a fine read; the teaching is never dogmatic, always stressing the need for versatility in fishing situations. The anecdotes, which also lack any hint of pretension, make the angling come to life. One delightful incident involves a box full of flies that fell into the river. The flies drifted over a school of rising trout, and the results of that "hatch" are enough to intrigue any fisherman.

This book, of course, joins many other works with the same purpose. My favorites include *Teach Your Dad How To Fish*, an out-of-print and undiscovered classic for young and old beginning anglers, by Burr Smidt; the whimsical *Curtis Creek Manifesto*, which is as informative as it is funny, by Sheridan Anderson; and the complete *Fly Fishing for Trout* by Dick Talleur. But even with the fine titles available, there is a niche for *Fly Fisherman's Primer*. Maybe it is more straightforward than any other—and this is meant as a compliment.

But really, there is no need to trust my opinion. Give this book to a group of beginning fly fishermen and give other books to other groups. Then see how much the different groups learn from the various texts without any help from instructors— and this is important. The final results might surprise some people, but they will not surprise me. The authors of the *Fly Fisherman's Primer* have a record of past successes in such contests.

— Gary LaFontaine
Deer Lodge, Montana, 1985

Fly Fisherman's
Primer

INTRODUCTION

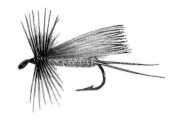

Fly-fishing is the joy of joys! It transcends the societal barriers of age, status, and wealth.

Don and I would like to start off by saying that fly-fishing is really very simple—we'd like to, but honesty precludes it. Let us hasten to add, though, that the individual areas involved in the pursuit aren't difficult; it's just that fly-fishing encompasses so many different subjects that to be completely knowledgeable one must pursue it for a lifetime.

Our intent is for me to provide enough written information and for Don to provide enough visual information so that you will be able to select your tackle intelligently and assemble it correctly, to read water effectively, and to cast well enough to take your first fish on a fly. From that point on, we have no worries. When you experience the anticipation and then the realization of that first strike, you will rush headlong to learn all there is to know about the sport.

In order to fly-fish well, you must touch upon all of the areas that make up the complete sport: the study of insects that trout feed on (entomology), fly-casting, fly-tying, the study of freshwater habitats (limnology), fishing techniques, and, not least of all, the history and lore of the sport. Any one of these areas can become so engrossing that it develops into a hobby of its own. We strongly recommend that you become familiar with the

terms mentioned in this book by reading through the Glossary (page 136); later you can use it as a reference.

We have books in our libraries that are devoted entirely to just one fly-fishing subject. Leeson's and Schollmeyer's *The Fly Tier's Benchside Reference* (Frank Amato Publications, 1998) devotes over 400 pages to just fly-tying techniques, for example! Our good friend Gary LaFontaine spent 10 years conducting research for his book *Caddisflies* (Nick Lyons Books, 1981); 336 pages devoted to just one family of aquatic insects!

When you begin, it is enough to only draw from the basics of each interest, but as you progress, you will find areas that are of sufficient interest to cause you to pursue them in depth. We know fly fishers who have become so enamored of fly-tying that they rarely actually fish anymore.

For us, the real pleasure has been in starting others in fly-fishing and fly-tying. As professional fly-fishing guides we teach a lot of beginners and each time that we help a new fly fisher get started we experience a renewal of our own interest and a sense of awe as to how much there is to be learned. Our only wish is that we could be there when each of you feels the throb of your first trout on the rod—know that we are with you in spirit. And if our methods have helped you to arrive at that point, then we have succeeded in our goal.

Fly-fishing is not just another method of catching fish. The fly fisher must be aware of everything from the cycles of the seasons to the life cycles of the insects. And in the beautiful settings where trout are pursued, it's easy to get sidetracked. All experienced fly fishers can tell of the times they missed good fish because they were distracted by the surroundings. I've missed several rises to my fly because I was watching an eagle instead of my fly. I have discovered Don sitting on the bank watching swallows taking hatching mayflies, oblivious to the trout that were taking them also.

We hope that you will choose to become a "complete" fly fisher, that is, one who is deft at all methods of taking fish on a fly. We know many nymph fishers who are exceptional fish catchers; they can take trout in numbers virtually every time they go out. They are restricted, however, to fishing certain types of water using only one technique; some can't even cast a fly line. Or, as one of them told a friend of ours, "You don't have to be able to cast to catch fish." If that same fish catcher would widen his horizons to include the other forms of fly-fishing, he could expand his enjoyment of the sport a hundredfold.

We also know fly fishers who will only fish dry flies. If they can't take trout on dries, they don't fish because that is the only type of fly-fishing that they have mastered. Again, those fishermen are missing so much of the pleasure to be had when astream.

Each of you will probably find a particular form of fly-fishing that will give you more pleasure than others, and there is nothing wrong with fishing only dries, or nymphs, or streamers — if that is your choice. But to be restricted to only one form of the sport because you simply haven't learned the other skills is cheating yourself.

You will find the vast majority of fly fishers to be truly friendly and interested in helping the beginner. Don't hesitate to take advantage of their expertise. There is much to be learned simply by watching a good fly fisher in action. Watch the casting technique, see if you can judge where he is going to lay the next cast, and pay attention to how he handles the line on the water and plays a hooked fish.

Above all, ask questions! We who feel that we have some expertise in the field are eager to share it with others. But each of us has developed personal preferences on everything from the choice of equipment to fly selection and casting method, and you might be bombarded with conflicting advice. Keep an open mind. Try it all and select the methods that work best for you.

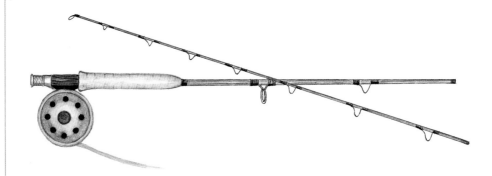

EQUIPMENT

Probably the toughest (and most enjoyable) step in getting started in fly-fishing is the selection of your first outfit. There are five essential pieces that you must have before you can even begin to fly-fish: rod, reel, line, leader, and fly. We will discuss each of the five items separately and in some detail in this chapter. But more important than any one of the five pieces is their relationship to each other. An outfit in which all the parts work together in a comfortable, efficient way is called a "balanced" outfit. This interaction of all the parts is what makes fly-fishing possible.

Having a balanced outfit isn't the only consideration, though. A perfectly balanced tarpon outfit is hardly what you would want to use, day in and day out, on a small stream in the Catskills, nor would a light trout setup, which might be perfect on that small stream, suit you very well if you were pursuing silver salmon in Alaska. That, then, is the starting point for making the selection of your first fly-fishing tackle—what type of fly-fishing will you be using your outfit for most of the time?

Although we can provide some basic background material to help you with the final decision, we have no way of knowing where and for what you'll be fishing. Your best source of help and advice is your local fly shop! The proprietor has an extensive knowledge of the area, knows most of the local fly fishers and the methods and equipment they prefer. Don't pass too quickly over the importance of that last qualifier, "methods and equipment they prefer." You're going to be nervous enough the first few times on the stream without the added pressure of having equipment that is different from what you see others using.

Surprisingly, to most beginners, the selection of a fly-fishing outfit starts not with the rod, as you might expect, but with the choice of a line weight. Unlike other types of fishing, when we cast a fly, the "lure" or "bait" that we are using isn't heavy enough to flex the rod, store energy in it, and then be cast by releasing that energy. The only thing that we have to cast is the weight of the line, and it is critical that the weight of the line be sufficient to store maximum energy in the rod for release during the cast, without flexing the rod beyond the point where it can recover and return the energy to the line for the cast. So, you can't select a rod until you know what line weight you need, and that's a function of where you fish and, to a limited degree, your personal preference. Let's first take an in-depth look at fly lines, and then we'll talk about your selection of line weight.

Fly Lines

The selection of a fly line can be absolutely bewildering when you are in the fly shop looking at an assortment of 20 or 30 different lines. The abbreviations L4S, DT6F, WF7F, and DT5F/S look like computer codes. How in the world can you know which one you need? The first thing we need to do is to crack the code. The manufacturers of fly lines have agreed on a set of standards for all fly lines produced in the United States. The first letter or letters in the code indicate the physical shape of the line from end to end. The letter L designates a level line; DT means that it is a double-tapered line; WF stands for weight-forward; and ST means that it is a shooting taper. We'll talk about what each of the designations means a little later.

The number in the code indicates the line weight in an indirect way: the weight (in grains) of the first 30 feet of the line determines the

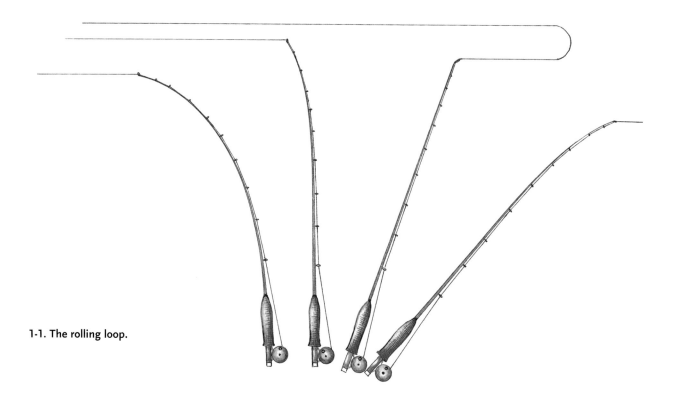

1-1. The rolling loop.

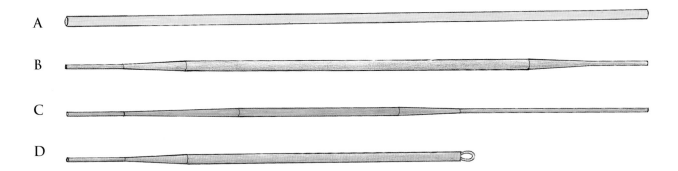

A

B

C

D

weight designation of the line. For example, the first 30 feet of a 7-weight line must weigh between 177 and 193 grains, a 5-weight line between 134 and 146 grains, and so on. Exactly what the line actually weighs is of no great importance to the fly fisher, though what is critical is that the line-weight designation in the code matches the one on the rod. Virtually all rods produced in the last 40 years are marked, usually just forward of the handle, with their appropriate line weight. If you end up with an older, unmarked rod, the owner of the fly shop can tell you what line weight you should use.

The last letter or letters in the code indicate the function of the line: F means that it is a floating line; S stands for sinking; F/S designates a floating/sinking line, that is, a floating line with a 10- or 20-foot tip section that sinks; an I (intermediate) indicates that the line will float if treated with a floatant and will sink very slowly if it is not treated.

So far it shouldn't be too confusing. A line marked DT6F means that it is a double-tapered, 6-weight (152 to 168 grains), floating line; an L4S tells us that it is a level, 4-weight, sinking line. Now we know what the code means, but we still don't have all the information we need to decide on a line around which to build our outfit.

Let's go back and plug in some more information to help us with our selection.

Before we begin to discuss what the different tapers mean, it's important that you know why we use tapered fly lines. As a fly line is cast, it takes the shape of a rolling loop. The energy imparted from the rod is expended as it "rolls" the loop forward, and if the energy is to sustain the loop until the line is unrolled, the line needs to decrease in weight as we progress towards the tip. A tapered fly line decreases in diameter (and weight) so that we get a smooth transfer of the rod's energy through the entire length of the line being cast. This transfer of energy is controlled by the manner in which the line is tapered (Illus. 1-1).

LINE SHAPES

You'll remember that we said there are four common tapers, or end-to-end shapes, of fly lines: double-taper (DT), weight-forward (WF), level (L), and shooting taper (ST) (Illus. 1-2).

Double-taper

A double-tapered line is cigar-shaped. The 70 feet or so in the middle of the line are of an even, relatively large diameter (the actual diameter will be determined by line weight); the next sections of approximately 9 feet on each side of the middle section taper quickly to a much smaller diameter; and the last 6 to 12 inches at each end compose the small-diameter tip section. Most manufacturers make their double-tapered lines 30 yards long.

The double-tapered line may be the best choice for the beginning fly fisher for one very simple reason: the line is identical from the center to each end. This means that when one end gets worn you can switch it end-for-end on the reel and, essentially, have a new line. The first year or so (while your casting may leave a little to be desired), the casting end of your line will take a beating, but with a double-tapered line you can then reverse it and still have a good line for the next several years.

Weight-forward

The weight-forward taper has the heavy, thick section of the line moved away from center and towards one end. A typical weight-forward line is designed with a 60- to 65-foot section of small-diameter line that attaches to the reel; it tapers for 6 feet or so to the maximum diameter, which is about 25 feet long, and then it tapers for approximately 12 feet to the fine-diameter, 12- to 24-inch tip section.

As mentioned earlier, the weight-forward taper has become the most popular line type. Its biggest advantage is that the weight of the line increases more quickly than the weight of a double taper. Thus, there is enough line weight to flex the rod and store energy in it with less line past the rod tip. Also, the tapered-tip section is longer than that of a double-tapered line, allowing for less disturbance near the fly when the line lands on the water.

There have been a bewildering number of special taper lines introduced by the manufacturers in the last few years: bass taper, rocket taper, nymph taper, pike taper, bonefish taper, distance taper, wind taper, and a plethora of others. The bottom line is that they are all weight-forward lines with minor variations in the placement of the thicker section of the line. A regular weight-forward line will serve 90% of your fishing needs.

Shooting taper

The shooting taper is a special line designed for long casts. Instead of transferring the casting energy throughout the entire length of the line to be cast, the shooting taper is just long enough to form a good casting loop. Another section of small-diameter line, called running line, is attached to the back of the shooting taper and is pulled along behind the shooting taper at the completion of the cast. Nylon or Dacron braided lines, or small-diameter (1- or 2-weight) level fly lines are commonly used as running lines. The shooting taper is usually only 30 feet long with approximately 24 feet of large-diameter line and 6 feet of tapering tip.

Level line

As the name implies, a level fly line is the same diameter from end to end. If you recall our original discussion about why we use tapered fly lines, you will understand that a level fly line is darn inefficient—you're right! The only good thing that we can say about a level line is that it is cheap, which doesn't necessarily make it a good buy. Level lines are generally just plain worthless for general fly-casting.

Level lines are great as running lines, and if you have infrequent use for a sinking line and don't need to cast it very far, a level sinking line might get you by. However, don't buy a level line as your first fly line!

FUNCTIONS

Let's skip the line weight discussion for a minute and go on to the last part of the line designation: floating (F), sinking (S), sinking tip (F/S), or intermediate (I). What you want here is strictly a function of planned use, and probably 95% of the time a floating line will best suit your needs. Generally speaking, all the others are special-use lines.

There is a stretch of the North Platte River in Wyoming called the Miracle Mile. Really big brown trout move up the river from a lake to spawn in the fall, and the river is large, deep, and fast moving. The most effective way to entice them to strike is to run large streamers through the spawning beds, right down on the bottom. An extra-fast-sinking line is the only way you can get the fly down to where the trout are. A sinking line is a real pain to use, though, because the drag of all the line under the water is so great that you must strip nearly all of it back in before you can pick it up with the rod and start casting again.

There's a lake that we discovered a few years ago that had been stocked with cutthroats. Although the "cuts" had only been in there two years, they ran 2 to 3 pounds. As indicated by the growth rate, the lake was teeming with food, mostly in the form of mayflies. When standing out in the lake, you could look into the water at any time and see myriad mayfly nymphs swimming towards the surface, settling back towards the bottom, and swimming back up. This cycle was repeated over and over in a jerky, undulating motion, as the insects made their way to the surface. Rapidly stripping in a 10-foot, sinking-tip line was the only consistently effective method we found for duplicating the insects' movement. In many cases, a 10- or 20-foot sinking tip will give you all the depth that you need when fishing

subsurface. It is also much nicer to cast and handle than a full sinking line, since you only have the short sinking section below the water's surface.

Although they sound ideal, intermediate fly lines are not very practical. They must be treated with fly floatant in order to float, and to keep them floating, you must re-treat them every few casts. If left untreated, they will sink, but their sink rate is so slow that they aren't that much different from a floating line. As with any compromise, an intermediate fly line doesn't accomplish either of its intended purposes very well.

So, unless most of your fishing is going to require one of the special-use lines, your first line should be either a weight-forward or double-tapered floating line. Now all that's left is to go back and fill in the middle of the line code, which designates weight. I've intentionally put off this part of the discussion because whatever recommendation we make, we are going to be wrong as far as some other anglers are concerned.

LINE WEIGHT

There are several considerations when choosing a line weight for your basic outfit, not the least of which is: what do the people that you fish with use? In most cases, they have probably chosen a particular line weight because it best fits the local type of fishing. Again, your fly shop can provide some sound advice in this area.

By far the most commonly used line is a 5-weight. Not too many years ago, this would have been considered on the light side, particularly in areas where wind is a common factor. Advances in both line and rod technology have made casting so much more efficient, however, that a 5-weight outfit is sufficient for most fly-fishing. Large water (i.e., long casts), commonly heavy wind, or the frequent use of large, wind-resistant flies might suggest going to a 6- or even 7-weight. On the other hand, quiet, small-stream fishing could be reason for going to a 4-weight outfit. Anything outside of a 4-, 5-, or 6-weight is getting into the area of special-use tackle.

Well, we're finally (kinda) there: most of you will need a double-tapered or weight-forward, 4-, 5-, or 6-weight, floating fly line. Discuss it with your fishing buddies and the anglers at the local fly shop. They probably won't all agree but their suggestions should all fall within the spectrum outlined above. The fact that they don't all quite agree only means that whatever you choose within their extremes will be workable. Your fly line is the most important piece of your equipment because that's what makes everything else work. Good fly lines are expensive but you're better off saving a few dollars on the rod or reel than to skimp on your fly line purchase. Besides, a good fly line will last for several seasons and the annual cost of even the best line doesn't amount to a great deal over its lifetime.

Rods

Now that you have decided what line weight you need for your type of fishing, rod choice is the next step in assembling your basic outfit. The items for consideration are rod material, length, and action. To a lesser degree, you will probably give some attention to the handle's shape and type of reel seat. In order to understand the basis for making these decisions, though, it is important that you know just how a rod does the work in casting a fly line. By the way, that is one of the first things you need to be aware of. We cast the fly line, and the fly only arrives where we want it because it is attached to the line!

When we move the fly rod against the weight of the line, the rod flexes, and this stores energy in the fibers of the rod. As the casting stroke continues, the weight of the line keeps the rod in the flexed position until we stop the rod's motion. When we halt the movement of the rod, the stored energy is released into the fly line so that it unrolls in the direction of the casting stroke (Illus. 1-3).

The ideal rod would store the energy generated during the cast and then release 100% of that

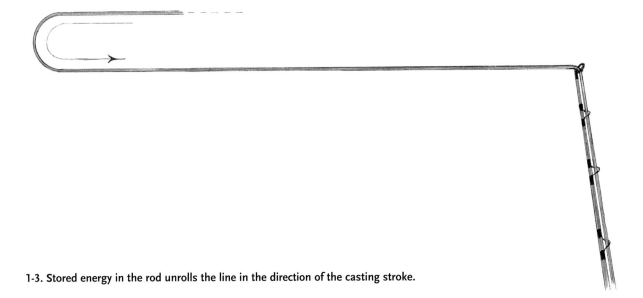

1-3. Stored energy in the rod unrolls the line in the direction of the casting stroke.

energy back into the fly line. Although no material can operate at 100% efficiency, the higher the efficiency of the rod, the less effort you will have to expend in making the cast. Efficiency, then, is one of the criteria we want to look for in making our rod choice. Although rod design has some effect on the ability of the rod to make an efficient cast, the material used in its construction has the greatest impact. We will discuss the pros and cons of the various materials just a little later.

The overall weight of the rod certainly has a major influence on how comfortable the rod will be to use. A fly fisher makes thousands of casts in a day of fishing. Even an ounce or two in additional rod weight can make a big difference in the number of foot-pounds of energy that you expend during each hour of fishing.

In much the same manner, the diameter of the rod will influence how hard you have to work to cast the line. The rod creates friction with the surrounding air as it is moved forward and backward during the casting stroke. And although this friction isn't great, it does become of some importance when multiplied by a factor of several thousand casts made during an outing, especially if there is a healthy breeze to contend with.

The shape of the handle on the rod is an often-overlooked point when considering the comfort of the rod. Certainly, you can cast with any size or shape of handle within reason, but if the handle is shaped in such a way that it fits the hand comfortably, you will experience less fatigue.

Another factor that you will want to pay attention to is what we call the feel or action of the rod. This is hard to define but is readily apparent from one rod to another and is primarily a function of the rod's design when comparing rods built of the same material. You will hear terms such as soft (or slow) action, fast action, and medium action. A slow action rod is one that

flexes and releases energy over a little longer period of time during the casting stroke than, say, a fast action rod, which feels as if it loads (achieves maximum flex) very quickly as the line weight is added and releases its energy very quickly at the completion of the cast. Again, the action or feel of a rod is very difficult to describe but something you will become quickly attuned to when trying several different rods.

There are many other terms for the action of the rod: hard, soft; slow, fast; nymph and streamer; or dry fly. Although they aren't as common as they used to be, you may hear them in passing. Don't become overly concerned because they are all arbitrary terms.

You will want to consider all of the above factors when making your choice of a rod, but the most important will be which material to select. Fiberglass, bamboo (cane), and graphite are the most commonly used materials today. We will look at the advantages and disadvantages of each.

FIBERGLASS

Fiberglass was the first artificial material that was really usable in a fly rod. The only other efficient material up to that point was bamboo (cane) and, although fiberglass lacked the "feel" of bamboo, it was very inexpensive in comparison and even offered some advantage through a reduction in weight.

Although you may occasionally hear someone expound on the great virtues of fiberglass as a rod material, it is decidedly second rate in efficiency. Even its low cost is becoming less of an advantage since graphite—a far superior rod material—has become as inexpensive as fiberglass.

Besides lacking the efficiency of graphite or boron, fiberglass also compares unfavorably in weight and required diameter. A fiberglass rod of a given length, designed for a certain line weight, weighs approximately 2½ ounces to as much as 4 ounces (that's one-fourth pound; multiply that by a thousand casts and you've moved an additional 250 pounds!) more than its graphite equivalent. It is also noticeably larger in diameter.

BAMBOO

Bamboo (cane) rods are still considered by most people to be the premier example of the rod-making art. Bamboo is the only natural material that really lends itself to fly rods, but the tremendous amount of handwork required to make a quality bamboo rod so inflates the price that it is simply out of reach for most of us. This hand labor, and the natural beauty of the material, are what make bamboo desirable. Its efficiency is somewhat less than graphite and, of course, it is much heavier for a given length and line weight than even fiberglass. Bamboo rods, however, do have a certain feel that makes using them a real joy.

Bamboo rods require much more care than rods built of synthetic materials. They aren't as efficient as graphite, they are relatively heavy, and they are very expensive. On the plus side, they do have an exquisite feel, are the most pleasant rods to cast, and are aesthetically the nicest rods that one can own. If you become a serious enough fly fisher that you can really appreciate the smoothness of bamboo and can afford it, you may well consider it in the future. We wouldn't, however, recommend bamboo as a good choice for your first rod.

GRAPHITE

Graphite rods are by far the most popular rods on the market today. They are very lightweight, small in diameter, extremely powerful for a given line weight, durable, and they can be designed to provide any type of action. All of the manufacturers market graphite rods across

a wide range of prices, with their older technology and less than top-of-the-line finish at the entry-level (least expensive) end of the spectrum.

Their top-end rods are built utilizing the latest materials technology and design characteristics available. They are the best their engineers can produce, at about double the cost of their entry-level rods. They are worth the extra cash if your taste and pocketbook run to top quality. Not only do they possess the best that ever-improving technology can provide, but the cork handles, reel seats, guides, and finish are all of the finest quality and combine to produce a rod that is truly beautiful as well as functional.

On the other hand, you can buy their entry-level rods which are nearly as efficient in use, without spending a lot of money. The biggest difference you will find is in the quality of the materials used to finish the rod: maybe an all-metal reel seat instead of an exotic wood, skeleton type seat; lower-quality cork for the handle, fewer guides, and less than perfect finish on the wraps. None of these items is likely to affect the use of the rod much, and most of them will cast a line as well as the more expensive models in the hands of a beginner.

We suggest that you purchase a quality, entry-level graphite rod as your first rod. Purchase the best you can comfortably afford because if you start with the cheapest equipment that you can buy, you are making the learning process more difficult. Instead of getting an honest feel for whether fly-fishing is for you, you will load the odds against enjoying it by making it more work and less pleasure than it can or should be.

COMPOSITES

Several companies have produced rods combining other materials such as tungsten and boron with graphite and have gained some popularity, at least in the short term. These composite materials do seem to give some marginal improvement, particularly in the area of efficiency, but at a significant increase in cost. This is due, in part, to the fact that these models are always at the top of their line of rods.

Reels

Although the choice of a fly reel is probably not as critical as the selection of a line and rod, neither is it something to be dismissed as unimportant, as some would have you believe when they state that a fly reel is just a place for storing line. The reel plays a role in balancing out the fly outfit as well as in helping us control the line and, perhaps, the fish on the other end.

The improvement in the reels available is the greatest advance for the fly fisher since the advent of the graphite rod. CNC (computer numeric control) machining allows the manufacturers to quickly make the parts for a fly reel very accurately with a minimum of human intervention. This technology has increased the number of makers of fly reels enormously, thereby creating competition for your dollars in the marketplace — always a good thing for us consumers. This advance means that you can buy a high-quality reel without spending a fortune.

You have a choice among three general types of fly reels: classic single-action, wide-arbor (or mid-arbor), and large-arbor. All three styles are available with smooth, foolproof disc drag systems.

All three types are actually "single-action" reels in that there is no slip-drag system like on spinning reels where the line is pulled from the reel without the handle turning. The handle on a

single-action fly reel is attached directly to the spool and as line is pulled from the reel, the handle turns. Even though, mechanically, all three are "single-action" reels, the term is now more commonly used when referring to the classic style of reel we'll look at first.

CLASSIC SINGLE-ACTION FLY REEL

The advantage of the classic single-action fly reel is that it is the most compact of the three types. It also has that classic look of a fly reel and just looks right on a fly rod. Its compactness, however, is also its weakness. The spool has a small-diameter hub (arbor) that the line is stored on and that means that the line tends to take a "set" in small coils. The small-diameter hub also means that line retrieve is slower than with a wide-arbor or large-arbor reel. Although single-action reels at the high end can be as expensive as the other types, they are generally the style found at the least expensive end of the manufacturer's offerings (Illus. 1-4).

1-4. Single-action fly reel.

1-5. Ross wide-arbor fly reel.

1-6. Sage large-arbor fly reel.

1-7 Multiplier fly reel.

WIDE-ARBOR FLY REEL

Some manufacturers call this type of reel a "mid-arbor." The wide-arbor reel has a considerably larger diameter hub than a classic single-action reel; therefore the line has less of a tendency to set into small coils. The larger arbor also means that line retrieve is faster than with a single-action reel (Illus. 1-5).

Because the arbor is larger, the reel frame and spool are made wider in order to store the same amount of line as on the single-action reel. Consequently, the wide-arbor reels are somewhat bulkier and usually just a bit heavier than the classic style reel. Many fly fishers consider that more than a fair trade to get less coiling and faster retrieve.

LARGE-ARBOR FLY REEL

The large-arbor reels take this concept a step farther. They have a narrow spool that is quite large in diameter. This reduces the coiling problem to zilch and line retrieve is really fast compared to the other types. Because the spool is held in a skeleton frame, these reels are generally the lightest. They truly do look strange though, at least to those whose eye appreciates the classic look of a compact single-action reel (Illus. 1-6).

OTHER REELS

Multiplier reels

A multiplier reel looks much like a single-action reel although somewhat larger and heavier. Inside the reel frame is a gear train that allows the spool to turn either two or three revolutions each time the handle is turned one revolution. The supposed advantage is that you can retrieve line much faster when the fish turns and runs toward you. The problem is that when a fish turns and comes back at you there's no way in the world that you can retrieve line fast enough to keep up—even at a retrieval speed of 3 to 1. There are only a couple of companies that still make multiplier reels. The advent of wide-arbor and large-arbor reels, which have just as fast a retrieve without the added bulk and weight of a multiplier, has pretty much eliminated multiplier reels from the marketplace (Illus. 1-7).

1-8. Anti-reverse fly reel.

Anti-reverse reels

The anti-reverse reels are great when they're needed but normal trout fishing isn't the place. These reels have a heavy-duty drag system that allows the fish to strip line from the reel without the handle turning, much like a spinning reel. The cost of this is great, not only in cash outlay (they're very expensive), but also in bulk and weight. If you're after tarpon, large salmon, or blue-water monsters, the bulk and weight aren't much of a factor because you'll be using large rods casting 11- or 12-weight lines. When trying to tame real monsters they are almost a must but shouldn't be considered for your trout outfit (Illus. 1-8).

Automatic reels

An automatic fly reel has a spring attached to the spool that is wound when line is stripped from the reel, and there is a lever under the reel that releases the spring and retracts the line. There are several reasons that automatic fly reels aren't a good choice: they are very large (and ugly), very heavy, and will barely hold a full fly line and certainly no backing. You'll easily recognize one . . . it won't look anything like a fly reel. It's simple, don't buy one or even take one to use if it's offered for free!

Leaders and Tippets

A fly leader is the piece of monofilament line that you attach to the end of the fly line and then to the fly. This enables the energy of the cast to be transferred from the fly line to the fly. Believe it or not, it isn't at all uncommon for a beginning angler to come into the shop and ask how to get the end of the fly line through the eye of one of the smaller sizes of flies, or, to find that they are using a section of 4-pound or 6-pound monofilament line from the end of the line to the fly.

You'll remember from our discussion about fly lines that we use a tapered fly line to get a smooth transition of our casting power all the way to the end of the line. In the same manner, the selection of the proper leader is necessary to ensure that the power we have generated during the cast is transferred from the end of the fly line to the fly. Our leader is tapered so that we can continue that flow of power to the fly. This taper may be achieved either by tapering the monofilament for its full length, called a knotless leader, or by assembling a leader of several sections of level monofilament in decreasing sizes, called a knotted leader.

Other than the choice between a knotted or knotless leader, the fisherman must make a decision regarding length of the leader, which may range from as short as 3 feet to as long as 14 feet.

Finally, you must decide what size the end of the leader, called the tippet, should be. Let's take a look at each of these decisions separately.

LEADER STYLE

The choice between using a knotted or knotless leader probably isn't nearly as important as we think. Either type of leader is perfectly capable of continuing the transfer of power from the fly line to the fly and laying the fly out smoothly. You may, however, hear some vehement arguments on both sides of the question.

For the most part, the proponent of knotted leaders is not arguing for off-the-shelf leaders prepared by a manufacturer. He is arguing for hand-made leaders that the fly fisher can assemble. These he deems superior to knotless leaders. Usually the argument is based on the fact that the angler has the option to choose from several different brands of monofilament, each of which has its own characteristics of stiffness or softness. The angler can then combine these into one leader to better control its performance: a hard, or stiff, type of monofilament is usually chosen for the section that attaches to the end of the fly line (the butt section of the leader) to pick up the full energy present at that point and to transfer it into the leader. Sections of softer monofilament in decreasing diameters are usually chosen for the middle section of the leader, and a limp, or very soft, material is used for the tippet or end section that will be attached to the fly.

In addition to being able to use materials to their best advantage in the leader, they can adjust the lengths of the sections to help control the transfer of energy to the fly. It seems that each proponent of knotted leaders has his own formula for combining brands of monofilament and section lengths, which results in the "ultimate" leader.

On the other side of the argument, the advocates of knotless leaders will tell you that all of the hocus-pocus of knotted leaders is so much rot! They argue that a leader which is smoothly tapered from the butt to the tippet and which has no knots in between will obviously transfer power more smoothly than a leader with several knots and various diameter sections because the energy is transferred more smoothly. If the knotted-leader system is so great, why don't those anglers also assemble their own "ultimate" fly lines in a like manner?

Besides, all those knots in the leader create weak points (even a good knot decreases line strength by up to 50%), and those knots tend to pick up dirt and algae from the water. Probably their best argument, though, is simply that knotless, tapered leaders work very well. And why in the world waste time tying your own leaders when you can buy a knotless, tapered leader for the cost of a cappuccino?

What should the beginner use? It would be hard for anyone to argue that hand-tied, knotted leaders are so necessary to fly-fishing that the beginner must learn to tie leaders before he can fish! A knotless leader will serve you quite well, both at the beginning and forever if you don't want to be bothered with tying your own. As you get more involved in fly-fishing you may well want to try your hand at assembling your own leaders; it is really more of a hobby than a necessity, but it sure will improve your ability to tie good blood knots.

In addition to getting the smooth transition of power from the end of the fly line to the fly, the leader places the fly at some distance from the rather large end of the fly line and is less noticeable to the trout. Just how far will be determined by leader length.

LEADER LENGTH

The choice of leader length is primarily based on the type of fishing you do and the type of water you fish. Because the leader is so much smaller in diameter than the fly line, it creates much less disturbance on the water than the line when the cast is completed. Therefore, a longer leader means that the fly will land farther from the line's disturbance. But, because the leader is also much lighter than the line, it is affected much more by wind, and a leader that is too long is very difficult to control during the cast.

When fishing in fast, rough water where the surface is already disturbed, you certainly don't need a very long, 12- or 14-foot leader. On the other hand, when fishing in a flat, billiard-table-smooth pool, where the line creates a real splash-down, you have to make sure that the fly lands as far away from the line disturbance as possible.

If you fish a streamer in the deep reaches of a fast run, a long leader will cause the fly to be lifted up towards the surface by the water pressure instead of staying near the bottom, where you want it. In a perfectly clear, slow pool, though, a short leader may cause the fly to swim so close to the end of the line that it will be seen by the fish.

If all of this sounds difficult, keep in mind that we are discussing extremes. For the great majority of your fishing, a 7½- or 9-foot leader will work perfectly well, and that is our recom-

mendation for your first leader. We will discuss exceptions to this when we talk about the particular types of fishing in later chapters. All that remains now in choosing your first leader is to decide what tippet size to use.

TIPPET SIZE

Generally speaking, the tippet is the section of the leader that attaches to the fly. In the case of a knotted leader, it is very easy to define: it is the last section of monofilament, and the diameter of that section is the size of the tippet. A tapered, knotless leader is a bit more difficult to define since the monofilament is tapered for its full length, and there isn't a constant diameter in the end section. In this case, the diameter of the last few inches of the leader is the tippet size.

The letter X and a number are used to define tippet size, for example, 4X, 5X, 6X, and so on. The larger the number, the smaller the diameter of the tippet. This is easy to keep track of if you understand the simple formula for determining the X designation. An 0X (ought X) piece of leader material is 0.011 inch in diameter, and that is the starting point for determining sizes. By subtracting the diameter of leader material in thousandths of an inch from 11, we can determine the X size: a tippet that is 0.007 inch in diameter is designated 4X (11–7 = 4); a tippet 0.005 inch in diameter is 6X (11–5 = 6). By the same rule we can determine that a 4X leader is 0.007 inch in diameter by subtracting the X size from our base number 11(11–4 = 7).

Using the correct size tippet is of great importance, particularly when fishing dry flies. To illustrate why, we need to return again to the point we made about the tapered line and leader, which enable us to transfer the power of the cast smoothly down the decreasing diameter to the fly.

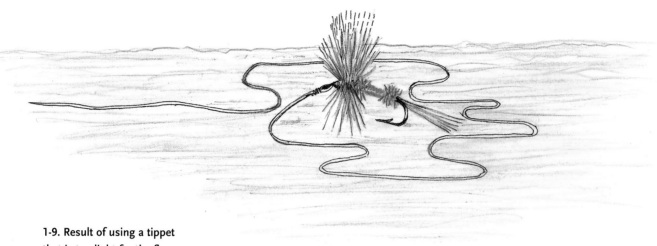

1-9. Result of using a tippet that is too light for the fly.

1-10. Result of using a tippet that is too heavy for the fly.

If we use a very small tippet and attach a large, heavy fly, we find that the fly line will unroll normally, transferring the remaining power into the leader. But as the leader unrolls, it will reach a point where the remaining tippet section isn't stiff enough to support the weight of the fly, and the leader will collapse into a pile on the water with the fly in the middle (Illus. 1-9).

At the opposite extreme, if we were to use a very heavy tippet and attempt to cast a very small, light fly, we wouldn't dissipate enough power through the line and leader. The leader would unroll so powerfully that it would completely overpower the weight of the fly, causing it to be turned over beyond the horizontal at the end of the cast. The resultant "kersplash" is guaranteed to spook every trout in the pool. It might even transfer enough remaining power into the fly so that it breaks through the water's surface (Illus. 1-10).

Determining tippet size isn't really that difficult, though. In most cases you can simply apply the Rule of Four. To find the needed tippet size divide the size of the fly by 4. For example, if you use a #12 fly, you would want a 3X tippet (12 divided by 4 = 3); a #16 fly, you would want a 4X tippet (16 divided by 4 = 4); and so on. If you use a #14 fly, you would want either a 3X or 4X tippet.

One last point about tippets, and it is important: the pound test of the tippet has nothing, let's repeat that, nothing, to do with the fly fisher. You will often hear a fly fisher, sometimes not even a beginner, state that he is fishing a 2-pound tippet, or a 2½-pound tippet, or some such thing, as if that tells you something. The pound test of a tippet is an expression of how much force can be applied to the tippet before it will break—nothing more! You can buy 4X tippet material with a breaking strength anywhere between 2½ pounds and 3½ pounds, depending on the type of nylon the manufacturer used in making the monofilament. You may well want to consider the breaking strength of the tippet when you purchase the leader, but, to get the leader to turn over properly with a given size fly, you must have a tippet with the right diameter (X designation).

Now that we have decided on a knotless, tapered leader, 7½ or 9 feet long, all we need to decide is what size tippet to use. If you will be fishing mostly #10, #12, and #14 flies, a 3X tippet would be ideal (the middle size, #12, divided by 4 equals tippet size in X). If most of your fishing will be done with #14, #16, and #18 flies, you would want a 4X tippet.

In practice, you don't change the entire leader each time you need to go from one tippet size to another. Your local fly shop has small spools of tippet material in all sizes from 0X to 8X, and you should carry at least sizes 3X to 6X with you.

Let's say you are fishing with a #12 fly, using a 3X tippet, and you notice a great number of smaller mayflies, about a size 16, appearing on the water. Instead of replacing your entire 3X leader, simply add on a foot or two of your 4X tippet material to the end of the 3X leader. If you need to go down even smaller, add a foot or so of 4X tippet and then some 5X to get down to the appropriate tippet size for #20s, or #22s.

To go the other way, from a smaller to a larger size, you simply cut back the leader (it tapers, remember) until you reach the right diameter for the size fly that you want to use.

You need to bring along tippet material for another reason besides being able to change the tippet to match the fly size. When you change flies, the knots you tie will use up sections of the tippet until your original 4X tapered leader becomes 3X at the end. To correct the situation, simply attach another foot or so of 4X material from your tippet spool. With a knotted leader, the problem occurs when you get to the knot where the last, or tippet, section of monofilament was tied on. The solution is the same: just add on another section from your tippet spool.

My technique for starting with a tapered leader is, before using it, I add to the leader a foot or so of tippet material that is the same size as the original tippet. This way I am reminded when I get to the knot that it is time to add some tippet. Otherwise, in the excitement of fishing, I tend to procrastinate, not adding tippet material until I've worked my way so far up the leader that I have to add two or three sections of decreasing diameters to get back down to the original size, practically making a knotted leader!

Flies

With the selection of which fly to put at the end of the tippet, we will have concluded our selection of the five basic pieces of equipment. If we could only provide you with a list of three or four flies that you will need, along with a short, easily understood explanation of exactly when to use each, we'd be all done with this chapter. If we could do that, however, we'd have to furnish those three or four flies in great quantities to all of the fly fishers in the country, and we'd be instantly rich and have no time to fish. It just isn't that easy!

Choosing a fly that a trout will accept is the single most difficult problem that the fly fisher faces. There are literally tens of thousands of fly patterns, and any one of them will work somewhere, at some time. The best advice that we can offer is to observe. Simply put, you want to select a fly that closely represents the insect that the fish are feeding on, or, barring that, a fly that most closely represents the prevalent food form.

Even this method doesn't always ensure success. Anyone who has been fly-fishing for long can cite numerous examples of instances when there were thousands of insects available to the trout, but when a fly was presented that resembled one of the insects in size, silhouette, and color, the trout ignored it. On those days the angler simply has to keep trying different patterns until something, anything, works. Most of the time, however, the trout feed on whatever food form is most available.

The food forms most available to trout are aquatic insects, minnows, and terrestrial insects or bugs. Additionally, crustaceans, such as scuds and freshwater shrimp, are often prevalent; worms of various sorts are taken when available; and, of course, the eggs of any species of fish are readily eaten. Of these, the fly fisher is most often concerned with presenting a fly that represents members of the aquatic insects since they are always available to the trout in his environment and do form the bulk of his diet.

The most important element of the imitative fly is, undoubtedly, its silhouette; it should have the same basic shape as the creature it imitates. Next in importance is probably size, and last is color. These aren't hard and fast rules, however.

Sometimes color is the "trigger" to the trout that our offering is to his liking, and nearly any fly of the right color will bring a strike. At other times, virtually any fly of the right size will work. In the majority of cases, though, at least these three elements must be correct to induce a strike. Another important factor is the material used in assembling the fly so that it will move in a lifelike manner when in or on the water.

In order to choose a fly to begin fishing with, then, the fly fisher needs to observe closely which type of insect is prevalent and to select the fly that best represents that insect. Getting down to the actual selection of which fly to use at a particular time is a complex decision discussed in much greater detail in Chapter 5. Also, see Appendix A for selected fly patterns. In making your initial selection of fly patterns, we recommend that you rely on the expertise of local anglers and shop owners. Keep in mind that as the seasons change so do the life cycles of insects and other food that the trout feeds on, and what worked very well for you in May may not even be worth trying in August. Keep in touch with the locals who know the streams that you are fishing and update your fly selection in accordance with their selections. It is a good idea for you to record which fly worked on which stream at what time so that you can develop knowledge of that area's fly needs.

That just about covers the five basic pieces of equipment that you, as a fly fisher, will need: rod, line, reel, leader, and fly. With those five items you have everything necessary to cast the fly and take fish, but there are any number of other odds and ends that you will want to carry along to make the fishing more pleasant and hassle-free. The list of additional items ranges from the almost necessary, such as a fishing vest, to gimmicks and gadgets that are one angler's necessity and another's refuse. We'll attempt to cover first those items everyone is most likely to want and then the items that we feel are simply luxuries.

Other Equipment
WADERS

Although you can fish some streams without wading, most streams require it. During a cast, the fly line travels the same distance behind the rod during the backcast as it travels forward during the forward cast. Trees and brush grow along the banks of most streams, so the angler must take a position in the stream where neither the forward nor backward cast will get caught in the foliage. Also, by being in the stream, the angler can change positions in order to make the best presentation of the fly. For the young and stouthearted it is possible to "wade wet," that is, to put on a pair of sneakers and plunge in. Up on the Middle Fork of the South Platte River, though, the water is only about 10 or 15 river miles from where the snow melts, even in July and August. No matter how young and robust you are, it is cold! The answer, of course, is to wear some sort of waterproof waders. The choice comes down to hip boots or chest waders.

Hip boots (Illus. 1-11) are much more comfortable than chest waders. They are lighter, cooler, much quicker to put on and take off, and cost about half as much as chest waders. Their main disadvantage is that they are always about 2 inches shorter than the depth of the water where you need to wade, regardless of the stream. You can't appreciate the thrill of ice cold water pouring down your leg until you've experienced it.

Chest waders (Illus. 1-12), on the other hand, come nearly up to your chin. It takes real bravado to get deep enough in the water to even approach flooding these waders. Chest waders are a bit awkward, heavier, cumbersome to don, and hotter than Hades on a warm summer day, although the advent of breathable waders has mostly solved this problem, but they aren't cheap. The best compromise, and what most anglers do, is to buy both hippers and chest waders.

I don't really mind the hassle of putting on chest waders if I'm going to be out fishing in a stream where I know I'll need them and if I'll be fishing for an extended period of time. If, however, I fish a stream for a while, jump in the car,

1-11. Hodgman hip waders.

1-12. Hodgman chest waders.

1-13. Hodgman boot-
foot chest waders.

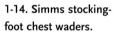

1-14. Simms stocking-
foot chest waders.

and drive to another spot to fish for a while, and so on, I don't want to be bothered with chest waders. It really is an insoluble problem.

If you must settle for one or the other, the best choice is chest waders, because then you can fish anywhere. You just have to accept the inconvenience of wearing them at times when "hippers" would be enough.

Whichever you choose to start out with, you must also decide what type of sole to get—ribbed or felt. Ribbed soles are fine for streams with sand or mud bottoms. But felt soles are a must for rocky, algae-covered stream bottoms. Wading Colorado's Frying Pan or Montana's Big Hole rivers in other than felt-soled waders is akin to playing Russian roulette with all six chambers

loaded. The bottoms of both rivers are composed of bowling-ball-size rocks covered with a thick layer of algae that is slipperier than grease. Felt soles "bite" into the algae, and the security of footing is really astounding. On the other hand, felt soles on mud or wet grass slide like skis.

You can also buy waders that have felt soles with tungsten steel studs mounted in them. They are especially good for walking on slippery rock. They are certainly worth considering if you will be spending most of your time wading in large, dangerous rivers. As the years have crept up on me, I find that I better appreciate the added security of studded soles.

You also need to choose between boot-foot and stocking-foot styles of waders. Attached to a boot-foot wader (Illus. 1-13) is a rubber boot, which is an integral part of the wader. The advantage of this style is that they are quicker to put on and take off than the stocking-foot type. The disadvantages are that they are considerably heavier, bulkier, and more expensive than a stocking-foot wader and, most importantly, the boot won't fit as well as a separate wading shoe, which can be laced to fit snugly.

As the name implies, a stocking-foot wader (Illus. 1-14) doesn't have a boot attached. Instead, a wading shoe is worn over the wader foot. An old pair of sneakers will suffice for a wading shoe in a pinch, particularly if you glue a piece of indoor-outdoor carpeting on the soles (Barge brand cement is the only thing we have found that always works).

Better than the makeshift sneaker, though, is a real wading shoe. Most come with felt soles (with or without studs) and are available in canvas, leather, or nylon. When you add the price of a wading shoe to the cost of the stocking-foot wader, you will have invested at least as much as if you had bought boot-foot waders to start with. The stocking-foot waders, however, provide a much better fit and are considerably lighter than the boot-foot waders.

VESTS

Unlike the boat or bait anglers, we fly fishers are always on the move, usually out in the stream. To have to return to the shore each time we want to change a fly, add tippet material, or put floatant on our fly would not only be annoying but would create unnecessary disturbance in the stream. Since fly-casting requires the use of both hands, carrying a tackle box is impractical, so we wear a fishing vest (Illus. 1-15). Selection of a vest isn't critical to the taking of fish, but choosing a good

1-15. Wm. Joseph fly vest.

one will certainly add to your enjoyment on the stream. Choosing a vest brand and type is a personal matter, but there are some things you should consider.

Most brands of vests are cut slightly oversize so that if you wear a medium-size shirt, a medium-size vest will fit over your shirt and maybe a light jacket. If you do a lot of early spring and late fall or winter fishing, you probably want one size larger so it will fit over heavier clothing.

For heaven's sake, don't buy the cheapest vest that you can find. Most of us fill our vests to overflowing (mine feels like it weighs 40 pounds at the end of the day), and a cheap one simply won't stand the strain. Zippers are expensive, particularly good ones, and a vest has lots of zippers. Guess where the manufacturer of a cheap vest first cuts quality to keep the price down? Right, the zippers. They then break, which results in you losing a fly box with a week's wages worth of flies in it.

Number 306 of "The Fly Fisher's Great Ideas" states that you might want to make or have someone make the vest to save more bucks. Well, ol' buddy, just show a fishing vest to a seamstress

1-16. Fishpond fanny pack.

1-17. Wm. Joseph chest pack.

1-18. Fishpond chest pack with backpack.

and suggest that you'd like to have one made. After one look at the number of pockets, compartments, and zippers, that seamstress will most likely tell you where you can go to get a vest. A good vest is relatively expensive, but a really good one will last for years and years.

CHEST PACKS, FANNY PACKS, ETC.

Another approach is to wear a fanny pack (Illus. 1-16) or chest pack instead of a vest. These are designed with lots of pockets, and most people find they are more comfortable to wear than a vest. The chest packs (Illus. 1-17) often come with another pack on the back where you can carry your rain gear, lunch, and assorted other items. Some models have a fair sized pack in the back (Illus. 1-18) with room for a hydration pack, rain gear, lunch, etc.

FLY BOXES

In order to approximate the size, color, and silhouette of any insect the trout might be feeding on, the fly fisher must carry a relatively large number of flies. Fly boxes are designed specifically for this purpose.

The variety of available sizes and types is overwhelming. Fly boxes made of plastic or aluminum are the most common, but you also see some made of wood. There's even a type made of cloth and foam. Fly boxes needn't be very expensive, and most anglers usually purchase at least two. First, make sure the box fits inside your vest pockets. Most boxes are sized properly, but some are too large for vest pockets. These are not going to be of much use to you.

Second, be sure the box can hold the types of flies that you want to keep in it. Some boxes have been designed specifically to hold dry flies

1-19. Wheatley divided fly box.

1-20. Wheatley fly boxes.

without crushing the hackle. Some of these boxes (Illus. 1-19) are divided into compartments so that you can keep different types of flies separate; some have ridged foam inserts that the fly is hooked into so that the hackle is held up away from the bottom of the box; others have small plastic clips that the fly hooks into so the hackle is kept clear of the box.

Although all of these boxes were designed to protect the hackle, the latter two types have the added advantage of keeping each fly separate. The compartment-type boxes lack that advantage but, on the other hand, enable you to carry many more flies in the box. Again, the important thing to consider in choosing a box for dry flies is adequate protection for the hackle.

You could, of course, carry streamers and nymphs in the same type of box as your dry fly box, but since you will probably carry more than one box anyway, you may as well consider a different type for these. Because streamers and nymphs are fished beneath the surface, their hackle doesn't need protecting. Boxes are available with flat foam inserts that you simply hook the fly into; with magnetic sections that the fly

"sticks" to; with small, flat clips that anchor the fly; or with coil springs that the fly hooks into. Any one of these will be adequate, although we don't recommend the spring type because hooks tend to rust if put into the spring when wet. Occasionally, you will run across an old-style streamer case made of leather and lined with fleece. These are guaranteed to rust the hooks if you put your flies away while still wet because the fleece retains moisture around the hook. As a result, it is not one of the better choices.

In addition to the abovementioned types, boxes are also available with combinations of holding devices: clips on one side with compartments on the other, foam on one side with magnetic strips on the other, springs and clips, and just about any other combination that you can think of. Wheatley is the top of the line in fly boxes and they are really works of art. The workmanship is superb and they are well designed. Their only drawback is that they are very expensive. There are some copies of the Wheatley boxes on the market that, although not the quality of the original, aren't too bad at about one third the price (Illus. 1-20).

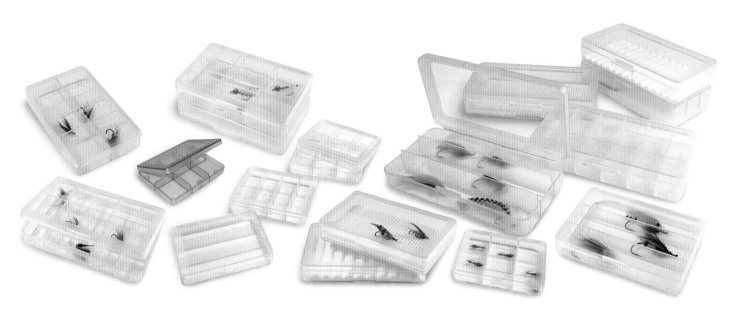

1-21. Millstream plastic fly boxes.

1-22. Nippers with zingers (retractors).

There are some really fine plastic fly boxes available in every style imaginable.

By the way, don't let the frail look of the plastic, compartmented boxes fool you. The good ones have riveted hinges and are tough enough that you can stand on one (Illus. 1-21).

By the way, dumping several dozen flies on the stream isn't the most humiliating thing that can happen to a fly fisher. Don, a friend, and I were fishing up on the Miracle Mile section of the North Platte in Wyoming one spring some years ago. I was out about as deep as I could stand up and was holding my dry fly box to change flies when I lost my balance. As I thrashed around to keep from falling, I dumped a couple of dozen dry flies on the water. We watched as the flies floated a hundred yards or so through feeding trout—without a single take. Now, that's humiliating!

NIPPERS

You must have some sort of tool for trimming off the ends of leader material after tying on a fly, adding tippet, or changing leaders. The simplest and cheapest is a large pair of nail clippers, which will do the job quite well. Like most other fly-fishing tools, you'll find some really nice nippers in the local fly shop or from the catalog merchants. Some of the small multi-tools are also quite usable and have the advantage of containing additional tools such as small scissors, assorted screwdrivers (worth a fortune when you have a screw in your reel or glasses that needs tightening), and files (Illus. 1-22).

FLY FLOATANT

When fishing dry flies, you must take along some type of floatant. It will waterproof the fly and assist it in floating. These floatants are available in small aerosol cans, plastic spray bottles, small plastic tubs, and soft plastic bottles. Most brands seem to work well, but the kind in the soft plastic bottle or tub seems to work best for us. Most are liquids or creams but there are a few powder types on the market, as well. By the way, floatants don't cause the fly to float, they simply temporarily waterproof the fly so that it doesn't get waterlogged and sink. The materials used to tie the fly, particularly the hackle, are the real means of keeping the fly afloat.

DESICCANTS

These are powders or small beads of material that readily absorb water. They come in small plastic bottles with snap-on lids. Drop your waterlogged fly in the bottle, snap on the lid and shake a couple of times and, voilà! You have a nicely dried fly ready to be treated with floatant and go back to work.

HAT AND GLASSES

A hat is one of those things that expresses individuality, so we aren't going to make any suggestions except one: your hat should have a brim all the way around to keep the sun out of your eyes in the front and hooks out of your ears on the sides.

You really should wear glasses and a hat to protect your head from windblown flies that will, occasionally, hit you while casting. Piercing your ear with a #6 streamer is sure to spoil your day, and catching a hook in the eye is too gruesome a specter even to think about. Glasses should have polarized lenses to cut down the glare on the water and to enable you to see below the surface.

LANDING NET

The experienced angler can land a fairly large trout without using a net and cause no injury to the fish but it's a skill that takes time to develop and an easier method is to simply carry a landing net.

You should carry a net with you, not because we all hook into such big fish that we need it to handle the monster, but because with a net you'll be able to land the fish much sooner and cause it less stress. Besides, the sooner you can land and release this fish, the sooner you can go for another.

Traditionally, the fly fisher has carried a small wooden net, which is still common practice on the stream. Also available are nets with graphite frames (very light and strong) and collapsible ones of spring steel. Which one you choose is unimportant but make sure that the netting is woven with small holes so that the trout won't get their gills caught in it and injure themselves. Also available are nets with soft rubber netting that is really kind to the trout.

There are myriad other gidgets and gadgets that litter our vests, some of which I wouldn't be without and Don wouldn't bother with. Thermometers, insect-catching and inspection tools, leader straighteners, forceps, knot tyers, and hook

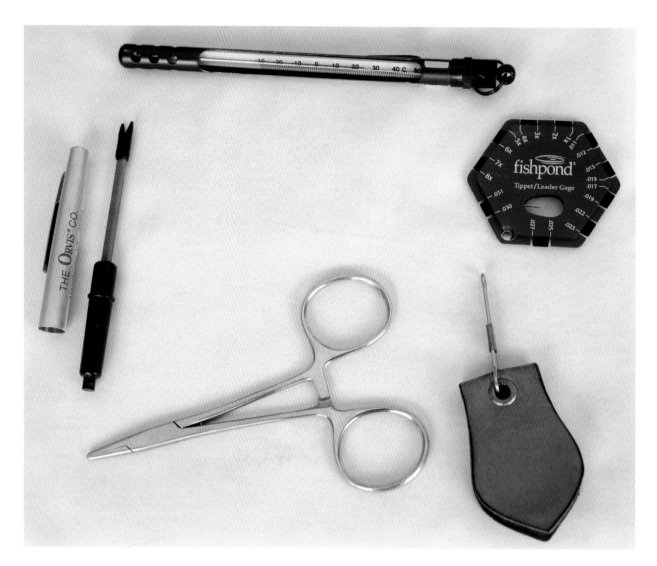

1-23. Clockwise from the top: thermometer, leader gauge, leader straightener, forceps, hook sharpener.

hones are only a few (Illus. 1-23). A small first aid kit is certainly worth having along. And one that you should surely consider buying is a leader gauge of some sort, for measuring the diameter of your tippet. It is necessary to add and cut back the tippet to match fly size. We suggest that you slowly collect these items as you perceive the need for them in your type of fishing.

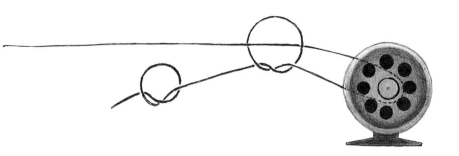

PUTTING IT TOGETHER

L et's assume that you have just returned from the local fly shop after selecting your line, rod, reel, and leader, along with some backing and a few other goodies that you are convinced are indispensable. After showing off all of your new equipment to the spouse and kids (and probably avoiding any discussion if not outright fibbing about what it cost), you realize that you need to assemble it into a usable outfit. This isn't a difficult task. In fact, it can be downright enjoyable, since this is the first time you have had a chance to thoroughly look over all the items.

That's important! You are going to develop a deep relationship with your equipment, and this is where it begins. Shops are always willing to assemble the outfit for new anglers but, to be honest, I would rather that the guy or gal did it. That way they wouldn't miss the joy of closely admiring the components while they put it all together. Besides, you are going to have to learn how all the pieces relate to each other, and this is the ideal time to figure it out.

Reel Setup

Let's start by getting the line on the reel. The first thing that you have to decide is which hand to reel with so that you get the line wound on in the right direction. Traditionally, the fly reel is mounted on the rod so that when the rod is held in the casting position with the reel hanging under the rod, the reel handle is on the right side (for a right-handed caster). Most reels come from the factory with the drag system set up for that method of operation. Since the drag on most reels is constant as you reel the line in and adjustable in the direction that line is taken from the reel, you will need to reverse the drag system if you want the handle on the left.

LEFT SIDE OR RIGHT SIDE?

It seems that half the anglers prefer the right side, the other half prefer the left. Let's look at both sides of the argument so you will have a basis for making your decision. Those who favor the handle on the left side say that they don't have to switch the rod from one hand to the other to reel in excess line, such as when the trout takes the fly after they have retrieved most of the line and have it piled around their feet.

The rebuttal from the right-siders is that the only time you should be reeling in line is when you move from one pool to another or when you go home. This is because the drag on a fly reel isn't like the drag on a spinning or casting reel, where the spool can slip and only a predetermined amount of pressure can be applied to the fish. If you have the fly reel handle in your fingers there is no drag; you have the reel held so that the spool can't move, and if the fish makes a sudden turn away from you he will probably break the tippet. Besides, if the reel has an external drag control, it is placed where you can reach it while playing the fish. But this position is only possible with reels mounted with the handle on the right.

The left-sider then replies that you don't have any business adjusting the drag while the fish is on anyway, so that isn't a valid point. Besides, he has seen several people lose big fish because they had several feet of line lying at their feet when the fish took, and the line caught on their foot or a rock and broke the fish off. If they had reeled in the slack when the fish first took, they wouldn't have lost it.

"Sure," says the right-sider, "but let me tell you about the time this buddy of mine ended up with skinned and bleeding knuckles when that big cutthroat decided to head for the other end of the lake just as he was reaching for the reel handle."

And so the argument goes, long into the night. Hey, both sides can make a pretty good case for their method, which indicates that it really doesn't matter much. From our experience (and we don't agree either, by the way), it would seem that whichever is the most comfortable and convenient way for you is the right way. If you have been using a spinning outfit for years, it will seem more natural for you to reel with your left hand. Just keep in mind that you don't play the fish with the reel when fly-fishing. The line hand holds the fly line, and the line is stripped in (or if the fish is small enough to be held, the slack is reeled in) or allowed to be taken out by the fish until all the slack is gone. Then he is allowed to run against the drag applied by the reel. Now that you've made that decision and have the drag system set up properly, you need to get the backing on the reel.

Backing

We put backing on the reel for three reasons: to give us something to attach to the reel spool, to fill up the spool, and to ensure that we will have more than 30 or 35 yards of fly line with which to placate a large fish.

If we didn't use backing, we would have to tie one end of the fly line directly to the spool, which would ruin a foot or so of that end. By using backing so that the spool is filled when we add the line, we create a larger "hub" in the center of the spool. This allows us to wind in our line much faster and keeps the line from taking a "set" of small curls. The last reason is one that we all wish we needed more often: the backing

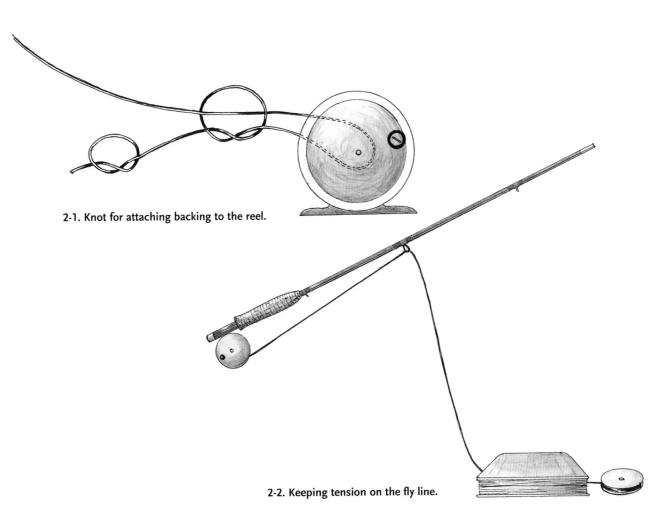

2-1. Knot for attaching backing to the reel.

2-2. Keeping tension on the fly line.

gives us extra line for fighting a fish. By the way, anytime you hook a trout capable of stripping line from the reel, you have a nice fish on. If the fish is stripping line from the reel while running upstream, you have a helluva fish on!

How many yards should you put on? If you are lucky, the manufacturer has included that information with the reel and your problem is solved. If this isn't your lucky day, the next best thing is first to wind the line onto the reel, attach the backing to the end of the line, and then wind on enough backing to fill the spool. Of course, everything is now on backwards, and you'll have to strip it all back off, reverse it so the backing is attached to the spool, and wind it all back on.

ATTACHING THE BACKING

The knot normally used for attaching the backing to the reel consists of a simple overhand knot with another overhand knot in the end of the line, so

that it can't pull through the first knot (Illus. 2-1). The actual job of winding the backing on the reel is made much easier if you put the reel on the butt section of the rod and run the backing through the first stripping guide.

If you don't have someone to assist by applying tension to the line, run the line through the middle of a large book, like a dictionary (Illus. 2-2), and wind the line evenly from side to side on the spool. You may well never get into a fish big enough to get down into the backing. But if you do, it's going to be a big one, and you're going to be upset if the backing gets tangled coming off the spool and your tippet breaks!

Now that you have the backing on the reel, you need to attach the end of the backing to the fly line. You have to be careful here if you chose a weight-forward line because, remember, the heavier section of the line is towards the front end, and it can be put on backwards. All weight-forward lines have a little tag on the end that attaches to the backing; that's the end you want.

There are several methods of connecting the backing to the fly line, but the nail knot (Illus. 2-3A through I) is the most common. Making this knot will probably be difficult for the first couple of tries but hang in there and get it right; you will be using this knot fairly often. In order to join the backing and the fly line, you have to tie this knot so that it is (1) capable of joining two materials that are very different in size, and (2) slim and smooth enough to pass easily in and out of the tip of the rod.

■ 2-3 A–I.
THE NAIL
KNOT.

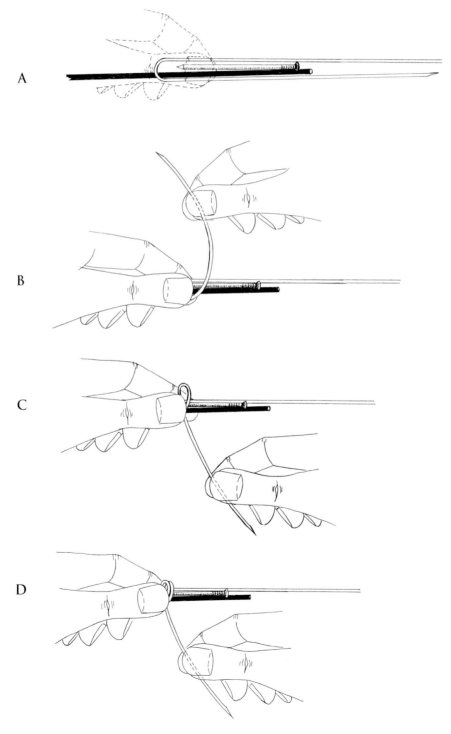

A

B

C

D

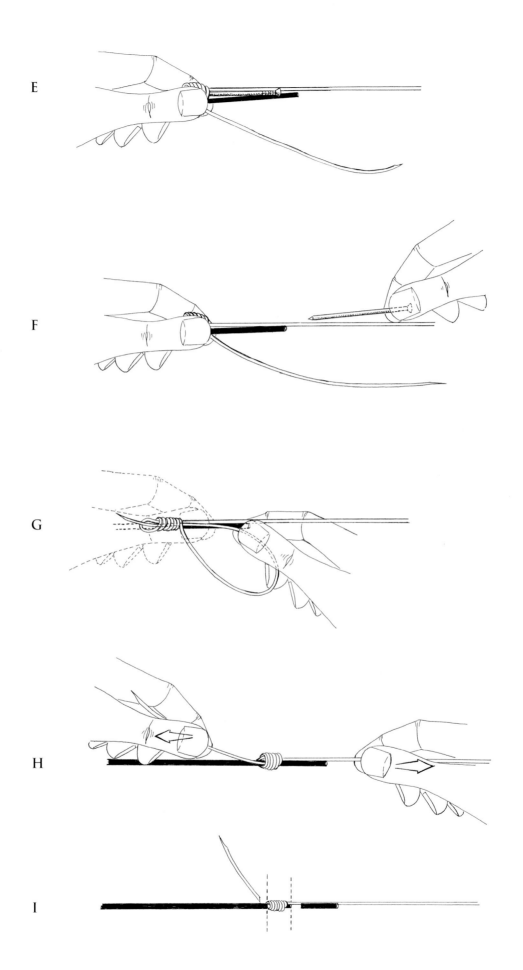

E

F

G

H

I

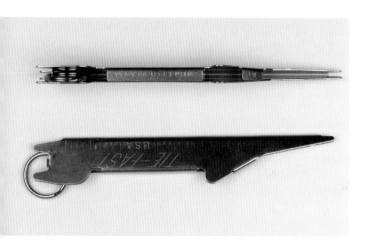

2-4. Tie-Fast knot tyer.

There are several different kinds of tools for tying this knot but we think the Tie-Fast is the easiest to use (Illus. 2-4). Even though the tool is great, you really need to know how to tie the knot without the tool so you can manage if the tool gets left at home or lost.

Nail knot

After you have tied a neat nail knot and trimmed off the ends closely, wind the fly line on the reel. Keep some tension on the line as you put it on the reel, just as you did with the backing. Once all but the last couple of feet of line is on the reel, attach the leader to the fly line. Use the nail knot for this connection, or one of the other methods appropriate for joining two materials of varying diameter, which will still produce a small, slim knot. Another good knot for this connection is the needle knot (Illus. 2-5A through E). You'll note that the knot itself is the same as the nail knot you used for the backing-line joint, except that the butt of the leader is inserted up through the inside of the fly line and out the side. Then the nail knot is tied. This produces a very small, smooth knot that slides easily through the rod tip and also decreases the tendency for the surface of the fly line to crack at the joint. This would create a hinge that might impede the transfer of energy from the line into the leader.

Epoxy splice

Another method is to use an epoxy splice (Illus. 2-6), avoiding the knot altogether. The butt of the leader is simply coated with epoxy cement and inserted inside the end of the fly line, which has been enlarged with a needle. This will give you the smoothest joint of any method, but I have seldom used it because the holding power of this splice may weaken over time, particularly if the line has been in use for long. Either of the last two means of joining the line and leader is superior to the nail knot, but both are rather difficult to accomplish while standing in the middle of the stream. In practice, you won't be changing the entire leader very often, and if you put one on at home, we suggest the needle knot or the epoxy splice. You do need to know the nail knot, however, so that if necessary you can attach a new leader while out on the stream.

Some fly lines come with a loop built into the end of the line, and this is the quickest and easiest method of attaching the leader. Many leaders come with a loop already tied in the butt section, and you simply pass that loop through the loop on the line, run the leader through its own loop, pull down tight, and you have a nice neat knot. The lines with a "welded" loop, that is, one that is made from the fly line itself, really work well. Those with the loop added to the fly line (usually made from monofilament) simply don't transfer the energy as efficiently, and they sink. We'd go back to the nail knot before using one of these.

The leader that you just put on will already have the tippet section in place. If you are using a knotted leader, the tippet is the last section of monofilament. If you are using a tapered leader, the last 6 or 8 inches will be the only part of the leader that is at tippet diameter because the leader tapers from the butt to the tippet, remember? There are a couple of knots that will work for adding tippet material to your leader when needed.

2-5 A–E. THE NEEDLE KNOT.

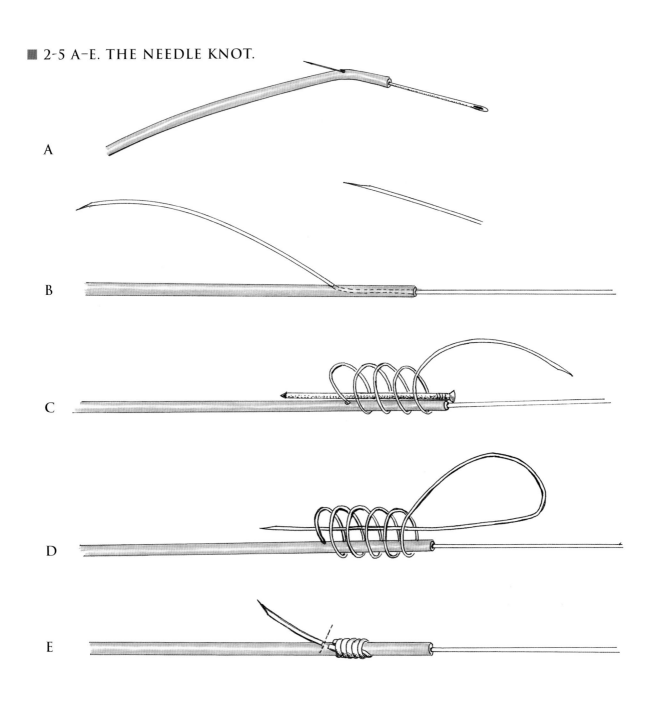

A

B

C

D

E

2-6. EPOXY SPLICE.

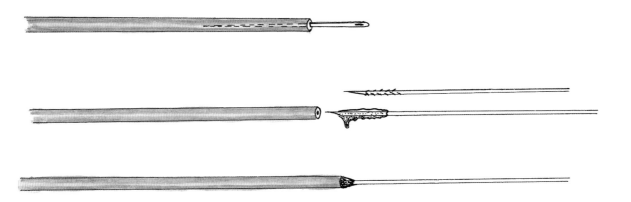

■ 2-7 A–I. BLOOD (BARREL) KNOT.

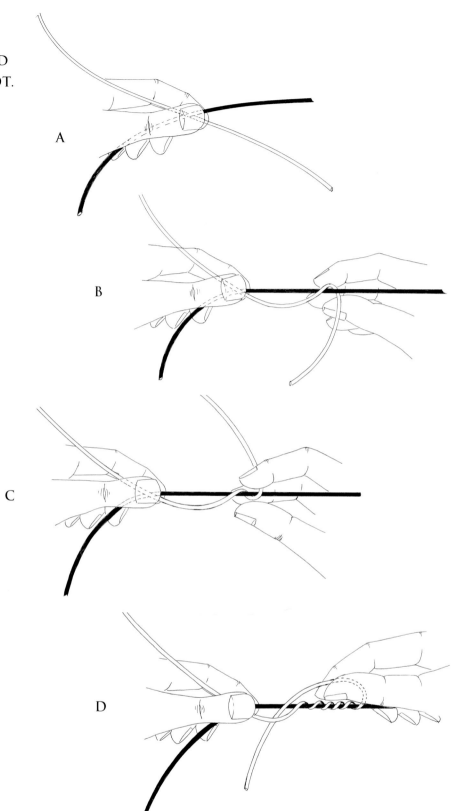

A

B

C

D

Blood or barrel knot

The blood, or barrel, knot (Illus. 2-7A through I) is the most common. With this knot, you can only join the tippet materials if they are about the same diameter; tippets more than a 2X (or two-size) difference won't work very well. Of course, you normally wouldn't jump more than one size anyway because that would disrupt the smooth flow of energy through the length of the leader.

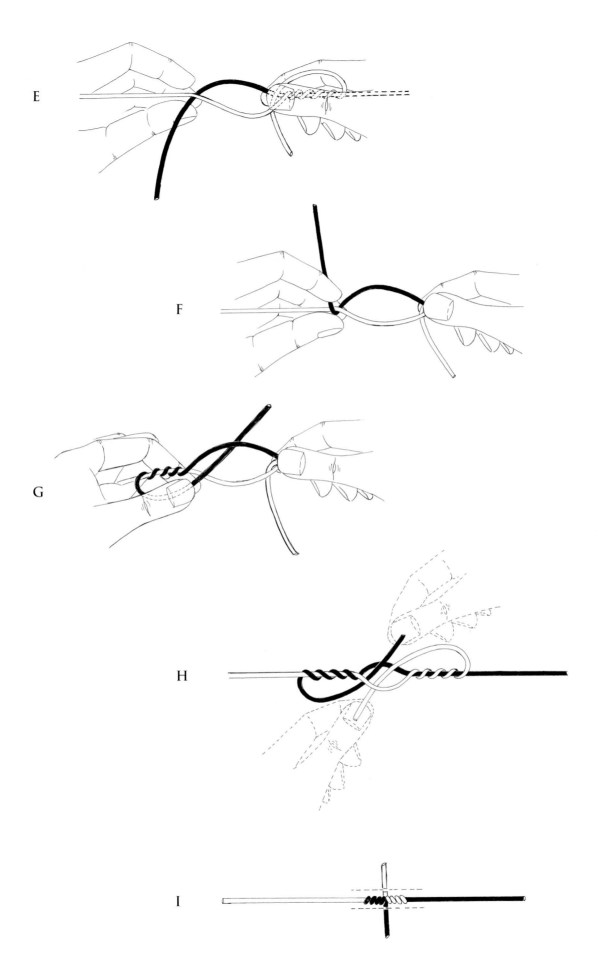

Surgeon's knot

The surgeon's knot (Illus. 2-8A through D) also works for joining the sections of tippet material. It doesn't make as neat a knot as the blood knot, but it's a good one to know since it's a little easier for most people to tie. That can be important when it's getting dark, your fingers are cold, or you're just plain clumsy. The surgeon's knot has another advantage; unlike the blood knot, it can be used to join sections of material that vary greatly in size.

Attaching the Fly to the Tippet

As you probably expect by now, there are also several different knots that you can use to attach your fly to the tippet. The clinch knot, the improved clinch knot, and the Trilene monofilament knot are the most common. The only one that we don't recommend is the clinch knot (Illus. 2-9A through E). If it is not tightened securely, it can (and probably will) slip.

■ 2-8 A–D. SURGEON'S KNOT.

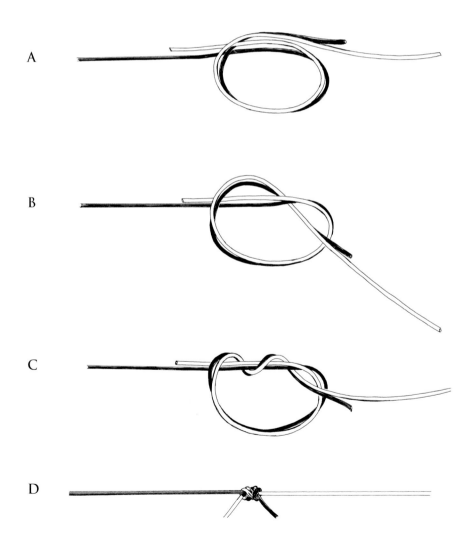

A

B

C

D

■ 2-9 A–E.
CLINCH KNOT.

A

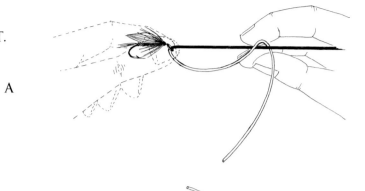

B

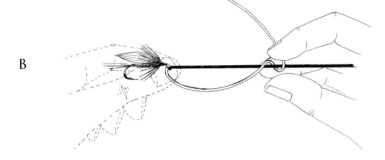

C

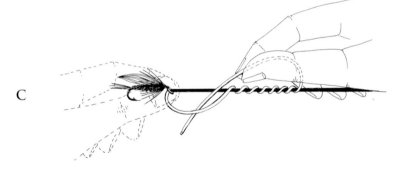

D

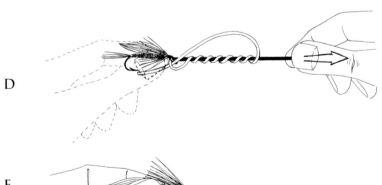

E

The improved clinch (Illus. 2-10A and B) is much superior and is the one that is used by most fly fishers. The Trilene knot, developed by the makers of Trilene monofilament fishing line (Illus. 2-11A through D), is very similar to the improved clinch knot but has much better knot strength, that is, the material within the knot retains a strength closer to that of the unknotted material.

Now that you have assembled your fly-fishing equipment, it's time to examine methods to get the fly out on the water. We sure wish we could tell you that casting is easy, but unfortunately there's quite a lot to it, enough in fact to devote the entire next chapter to the subject.

■ 2-10 A AND B. IMPROVED CLINCH KNOT.

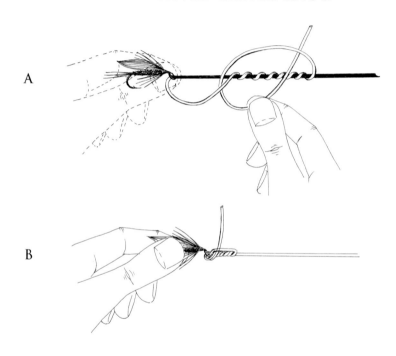

A

B

■ 2-11 A–D. TRILENE KNOT.

A

B

C

D

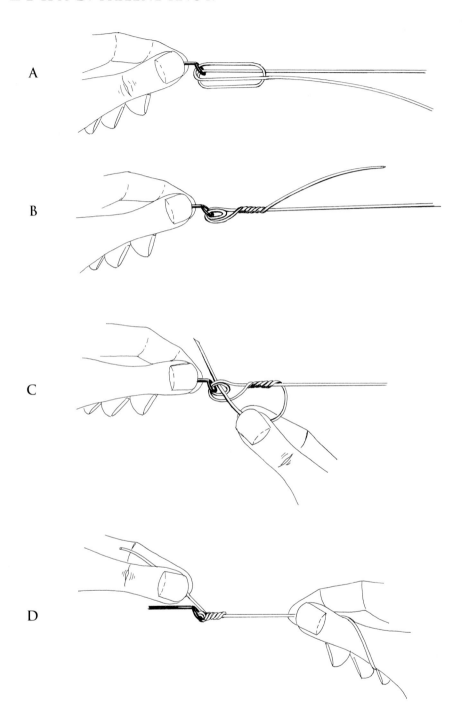

FLY CASTING

Developing the ability to cast a fly well is certainly the hardest part of getting started in fly-fishing. Not that fly casting is difficult; it's just different from any other type of casting. Through our many years of running fly-fishing schools and guiding, we've taught thousands of folks to fly-cast and I'm constantly amazed at how quickly people who have never done any kind of fishing pick up the basic casting stroke. Those who have been using a spinning or casting outfit for years are the ones that have a really tough time of it. I'll bet you're one of them, aren't you? Well, not to worry, we manage to get everyone casting after a couple of hours of practice. The reason those who have cast before take longer to learn is that fly casting is different, not more difficult, just so darn different. First, let's take a look at the basic physics involved in casting a fly line and examine how the whole system works. Next, we'll discuss the basic casting stroke. And with rod in hand you'll start practicing. And last, we'll get into the other types of casts that you will find necessary during your fishing ventures.

Casting Physics

Basically, you can think of the fly rod as a spring. As you move the rod against the weight of the fly line, the rod flexes even though the fibers in the rod want to return to their original position, or straighten out. They don't

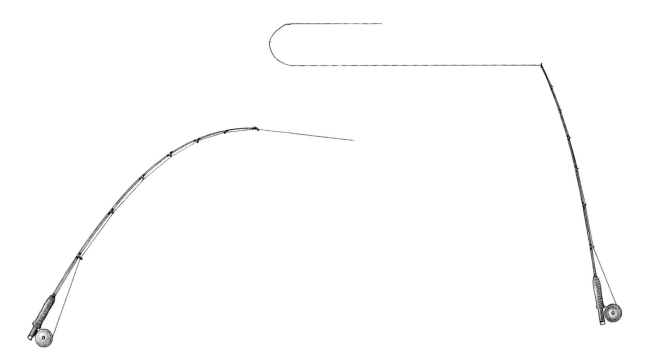

3-1. Rod flexing at beginning of backcast.

3-2. Rolling loop in line formed during backcast.

have enough strength to resist the weight you have applied to them, however, as long as you move the rod against the weight of the line.

If you pull the rod towards your body (called the backcast), the weight of the line will keep the rod bent, or flexed, in a forward arc (Illus. 3-1). When you stop the rod's rearward movement and impart a snap, the flexed fibers overcome the weight of the line and straighten. This straightening then accelerates the rearward movement of the line enough to throw it all behind you. The line forms the typical candy-cane shape (Illus. 3-2) as the section emerging from the rod's tip can't continue its movement, and the rest of the line continues its motion to the rear. The line is now formed into a rolling loop with a longer and longer section stopping its movement, while the end of the line moves closer to the loop.

If, as the line straightens, you move the rod forward, the weight of the line will flex the rod in an arc to the rear (Illus. 3-3).

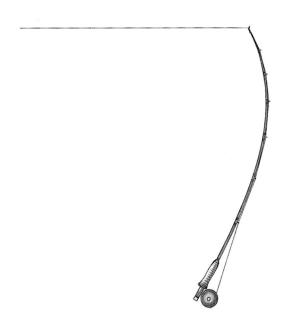

3-3. Rod flexing at beginning of forward cast.

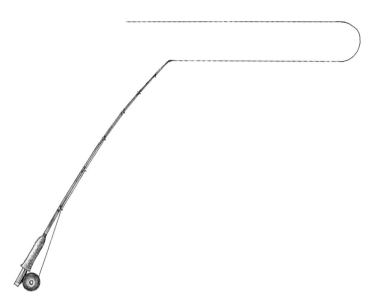

3-4. Rolling loop in line formed during forward cast.

Continuing the forward motion of the rod (we're now into the forward cast) will keep the rod flexed until the rod motion is stopped and the snap is imparted. Just as in the backcast, this enables the rod's fibers to attempt to return to their original position (straight) and will apply enough force to throw the line forward. The line will now form a forward-rolling loop (Illus. 3-4).

Casting Problem Solutions

Essentially, that's all there is to it! The problems that beginners have, though, are (A) getting the rod movement established in the correct plane; (B) stopping the rod at the correct positions; and (C) realizing (and remembering) that you must wait for all of the line to pass through the rolling loop and straighten out before you can start the rod movement in the other direction. These three problems are the bane of every beginning fly caster, particularly for those accustomed to a spinning or casting rod. Let's take a look at each of them, starting with the last one.

WAITING FOR THE LINE TO STRAIGHTEN OUT

You must keep in mind that the only thing you can cast is the fly line. The fly doesn't weigh enough to be able to flex the fibers in the rod.

If you were to strip off several feet of line into a pile at your feet and then start your rod movement, you would only be adding the weight of the line between the rod tip and the pile, which would not be nearly enough to flex the rod. In order for the line weight to be felt in the rod, the line must be straightened out so that its full weight is opposing the movement of the rod. This is where the long-time spinning or casting angler has a problem.

Unlike a fly, a lure or bait has enough weight to cause the rod to bend when you move it away from the weight. All you have to do, then, is let the weight hang off the end of the rod and then make a quick forward movement to flex the rod and start the lure on its way. When the forward movement is stopped, the rod snaps straight and applies additional power to the cast. In most cases, it's all done with a snap of the wrist. The timing, though, is critical. If you release the line even a few microseconds too soon, the rod releases its energy into the cast in an upward direction and you make a beautiful cast—straight up! If you release the line a tad late, the lure hits the water at your feet—traveling at about 120 miles per hour! That timing is a hundred times more critical than when fly casting, but, since you've been doing it for years, you aren't going to believe it at first.

You can't start the forward cast with a fly rod until the line has straightened out behind you. Let's repeat that. You can't start the forward cast until the line has straightened out behind you. If you do start forward while the line is still in the rolling loop, you will only accelerate the line movement through the loop. Remember that pile of line at your feet? If the line hasn't straightened out you get the same effect; its full weight can't be felt against the rod, and the rod won't flex.

Deciding when to start the rod movement for the backcast isn't difficult because the line is either on the water or unrolling in front of you where you can see when it straightens out. Knowing when to start the forward cast is so difficult because you can't easily see what's going on as the loop unrolls behind you.

An important point to remember is that the rod must stop at each end of the cast and remain motionless until the line has straightened out. Then, and only then, can you start the rod movement in the opposite direction. You can't wait too long, though.

Keep in mind that while the loop unrolls, gravity is pulling it down towards the ground, and if you pause too long, the line will go into the bushes behind you. So the important timing factor is that the rod motion must start between the time the loop unrolls and before gravity pulls it to the ground. Compared to the timing factor involved in releasing the line with a spinning or casting rod, we have an eternity. Really! With fly casting you can miss the timing by a half second or so and still complete the cast.

As we stated before, the difficult part is behind you, literally. Deciding when to start the forward cast is the hard part, because you don't have eyes in the back of your head. But you can turn your head, an action my students seem to have trouble remembering. The solution is easy.

Turn your head and watch the backcast so you can see what is going on. I think the problem arises because accomplished casters don't watch the backcast and beginners feel that they're cheating if they peek.

After learning to cast fairly well, you won't need to look either, at least most of the time. There's been a lot written about waiting until you feel the tug of the line (indicating that it has straightened out) before starting forward. Bunk! A properly executed cast, which isn't overpowered, just won't pull on the rod hard enough for you to feel it in the handle. Even if you do use more power than necessary and cause the line to unroll so strongly that it does tug on the rod noticeably, it still won't work. By the time the line straightens out completely, transmits its weight for the full length of the line into the rod, and the resulting rod movement travels the length of the rod to your hand, and you react—it's too late. Gravity has already pulled the line on or near the ground.

How then do you know when to start forward if you don't look? I'm convinced that a lot of it is "learned timing," that is, after casting for several hours, you will learn by trial and error when to start forward. This timing is strongly influenced by seeing half of the cast out in front of you, which should take the same timing as the backcast. I don't really know how long it takes the average beginner to develop this timing, but I do know that if you look at the backcast, it doesn't matter. Somewhere down the road you will suddenly realize that you aren't looking anymore.

You'll notice that I qualified the comment about the experienced caster not needing to look at the backcast with the words "most of the time." Sometimes your timing might be off a bit, and your casts just aren't quite right. The problem may be the wind either straightening out the backcast faster than normal (if coming from in

3-5. Start forward cast as the end of the line enters the loop.

front of you) or slower than normal (if coming at your back). The way to solve the problem is to peek, watch the backcast, and see what is going on so that you can adjust your timing. There is no penalty for looking.

So now that we've got you looking at the backcast, just when should you start forward? You should start the forward rod movement just as the end of the line enters the rolling loop (Illus. 3-5).

If you start the cast before that, you will accelerate the line around the loop. It will be traveling so fast that when the tip of the leader reverses into the forward motion, the shock will be so great that it will snap off the fly. If you hear a loud crack behind you, you know you started the forward cast too soon. That crack sounds just like the cracking of a whip. Each time you hear it, it means you've lost another fly.

On the other hand, if you wait until the line is completely straight before you start the forward

movement, you will be too late. By the time you see that the line is straight, go through the necessary thought process to tell the arm to move, and actually get the movement started, the line will have dropped several feet. So when we say don't start the forward cast until the line straightens out, we mean that to a certain extent you must anticipate exactly when that will happen.

If you watch for the end of the line to enter the loop, by the time you react the line will be just straightening out, and your timing will be perfect. You won't snap off the fly, and you'll be cheating gravity out of its opportunity to do you in.

Keep in mind that the time required for the line to unroll so you can start the opposite half of the casting stroke varies. It is directly affected by the length of the line: the longer the line, the longer it will take for all of it to move through the rolling loop. It is affected by how much energy you impart to the line: the more energy you impart to the cast, the faster the line speed will be. A wind in your face will cause the backcast to unroll faster than the forward cast made into the wind. And, finally, the size of the unrolling loop (which we will discuss later) will have a major effect on how long it takes for the line to straighten.

STOPPING THE ROD AT THE CORRECT POSITION

The second difficulty everyone has (again, especially the spinning or casting rod user) is rod position. If we use the hours on a clock (12 o'clock being straight up) to represent rod movement, you must stop the rod at the 11 o'clock position on the backcast and at the 1 o'clock position on the forward cast, as the caster looks at the rod (Illus. 3-6). If you allow the rod tip to move past either of these positions, you lower the rolling loop so that it unrolls towards the ground, and gravity will get it for sure.

Pick up the butt section of your rod and, holding your arm still, move the rod forward and back by flexing your wrist (Illus. 3-7). You'll notice that at the forward position of the wrist the rod isn't pointed much past the 1 o'clock position

but as the wrist is flexed to the rear the rod is pointed straight out behind you, or even slightly towards the ground. Now envision the movement of the unrolling loop in the plane where you have the rod pointed, and you can readily see the problem: on the backcast you are throwing the line at the ground.

3-6. Rod position at end of forward cast.

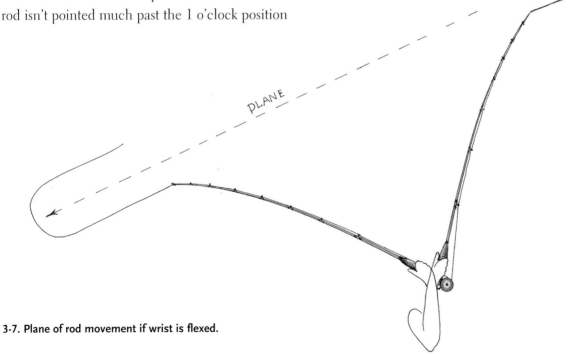

3-7. Plane of rod movement if wrist is flexed.

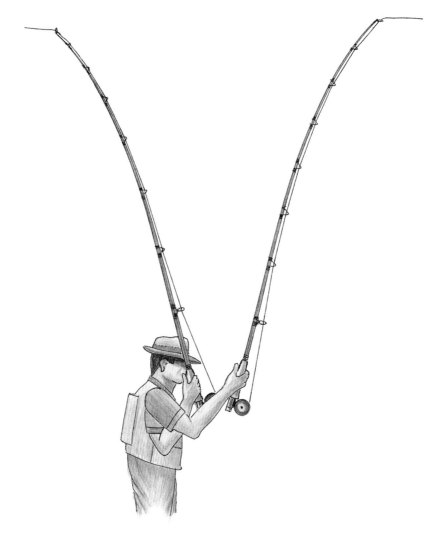

3-8. Proper rod positions on forward cast and backcast.

Because the cast with a spinning or casting rod is made with a wrist movement only, those who have been fishing this way for years must break the habit of making the cast with the wrist. It is truly difficult to overcome this habit because it has been so strongly reinforced over time.

In order to get a long enough casting stroke to flex the rod fully and gain enough time for the line to unroll completely during the forward and backward casts, you must make the cast with a pushing and pulling arm motion. Extend your arm fully during the forward cast, and on the backcast, drop your elbow to the hip so that your hand moves back and up slightly into a position close to the shoulder at the stop position (Illus. 3-8).

On the forward cast, straighten out your arm with a forward pushing motion and drop your hand a few inches. This slight drop of the hand during the forward movement comes naturally to most people.

The wrist snap at either end of the casting stroke is where many beginners have a problem. This snap is necessary for a couple of reasons: to lower the rod tip several inches so that the fly line can clear it (if the rod tip moved absolutely horizontal to the ground, the fly line couldn't help but hit the rod); and to "unload" the rod, or release the stored energy. The fibers in a rod do not possess energy in themselves; the rod isn't capable of propelling the fly line. It does flex during the casting stroke, however, which stores potential energy in the rod. When you stop the rod suddenly and snap your wrist, you release the stored energy in the rod. You get out of the rod only what you put into it. You can, however, control how slowly or quickly this energy is released by timing your wrist snap correctly.

Most of my students have found the following technique to be most effective: they make every effort to keep the wrist from snapping at all. Now before all you old-timers start screaming, try this exercise. Extend your arm fully with the wrist bent forward, as if you had just completed the forward casting stroke (rod at the 11 o'clock position). Slowly drop your elbow, pulling your hand back and up slightly towards your shoulder, keeping the wrist bent forward. You will notice that if you keep the wrist locked in the bent-forward position it is very difficult to move the hand the last 2 to 4 inches. At the point where it takes a conscious effort to keep the wrist from rotating back is precisely where the wrist snap should occur—at the end of the casting stroke, the point where you have the maximum flex in the rod.

Now, with the wrist cocked to the rear (rod would be pointing at the 1 o'clock position), start moving the hand forward and slightly down. Keep the wrist cocked and you find that it is almost impossible to extend the arm fully! Again, the wrist wants to rotate so that the elbow can straighten out the last 2 to 4 inches. And, of course, this last 2 to 4 inches of rod movement is where the wrist snap should occur.

I'm not telling you not to use the wrist; I'm telling you that if you concentrate on not making a wrist snap, your wrist will rotate automatically at the proper time simply because of the physiology of the arm—sure proof that we were meant to fly-fish!

It is also difficult to stop the rod at the correct position at the end of the backcast. It is very easy (natural, in fact) to overrotate your wrist so that the rod is pointed straight out behind you or even at the ground. This is difficult to correct, particularly for the long-time spinning or casting angler who is used to starting the casting stroke with the wrist fully flexed. This position allows for a much longer arc movement of the rod, but it won't work for fly casting when you've got 30 or 40 feet of line out behind you.

The best teaching aid that I have found for students who consistently over-rotate their wrist is a device called a Royal Wulff Wristlok (Illus. 3-9).

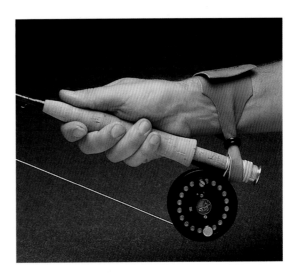

3-9. Royal Wulff Wristlok.

It is simply a double loop of leather; one loop wraps around the wrist with Velcro fastening tape, and the other loop wraps around the butt of the rod. The device serves as a link between the wrist and the rod butt and prevents the caster from overrotating the wrist on the backcast. You won't need one for very long because it will quickly establish the correct wrist position. It seems a shame to have to buy one, but it only costs a few dollars and is by far the most effective method for teaching your wrist to behave.

Although not as efficient, I've gotten by many times when teaching a beginner by using a simple Velcro strap around the rod butt and the learner's wrist. It is actually a little too restrictive to be completely effective but will overcome the overrotation problem.

MAINTAINING THE CORRECT PLANE

The third problem that nearly every beginning fly caster experiences is trying to keep the forward and backward casts in the same plane, or track. Many students tend to move the rod in a circular motion during the cast (Illus. 3-10). This circular motion creeps into the cast just about the time the student starts to cast well. It is an unconscious return to using the wrist throughout the cast. Even though the hand moves forward or back in

a straight line, the wrist rotates throughout the casting stroke, not in the direction of the cast but in a circular rotation; the entire arm rotates on its axis, the elbow. This arm rotation throws the rod tip in an arc out away from your body at the start, and back to a position in front of you at the completion of the cast.

The line, of course, must follow the rod tip, which means that it moves much farther following the arc than it would in a straight line. You waste a good portion of your casting energy by moving the line the extra distance. This problem is somewhat difficult to see by watching the rod tip, but if you look at your hand position at the completion of the backcast, you will easily spot it. If you move the rod in an arc during the cast, you will find that your hand is in an open position at the end of the backcast. That is, the palm of your hand, instead of your knuckles, will be facing forward.

To cast effectively, the hand and rod must move forward and back in a straight line. The track of the rod tip need not be absolutely vertical, though. In fact, that would be a very unnatural and uncomfortable plane to move the rod through. The rod can extend out from the body at any angle that is comfortable for you during most casts, and sometimes you might make the casting stroke horizontal to the ground. But whatever the

3-10. Incorrect, circular movement of rod when casting.

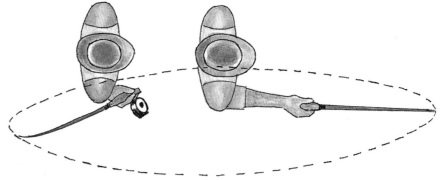

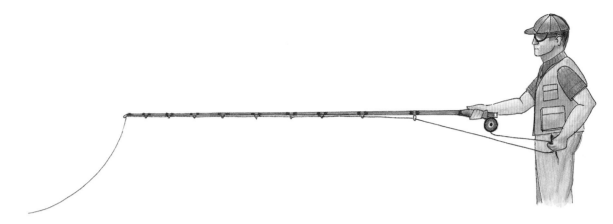

3-11. Line hand in pocket.

angle from vertical, it is important that you move the rod in that established plane during both the forward and backward casts. Now the time has come to grab your rod, head for the nearest open area, and start casting.

Learning the Basics

I'll give you casting instructions for a right-handed caster. You lefties will have to reverse them, but you're used to that, right?

It's possible to cast effectively when standing with your feet in about any position. But while learning, you should stand facing the direction of the forward cast, with your right toe about even with your left heel. Your feet should be about shoulder width apart. This position is important because with the right shoulder slightly behind the left, your body is out of the way of your casting arm. More important, this position makes looking back over your right shoulder easy, so you can see the backcast.

Hold the rod with a loose grip; squeeze it just enough to keep it from falling out of your grasp. This is important because if you keep your fist tightly clenched, you won't be able to straighten out your arm completely. Besides, if you keep all

your arm muscles contracted by gripping the rod handle tightly, you will tire very quickly.

Strip off 20 feet or so of line from the reel and then back up so that the line lies straight out across the grass in front of you. Now pull enough extra line from the reel so that you can hold it in your left hand with your thumb hooked in your pocket and the right arm fully extended. Point the rod tip at an imaginary spot about 4 feet or so above the line. Keep your left thumb hooked in your pocket for now (Illus. 3-11).

BACKCAST

To start the backcast, simply pull the reel quickly and smoothly to your shoulder. Notice that I said to move the reel, not the rod. If you think in terms of moving the reel in the correct manner, the rod will, of necessity, follow. This pulling motion should accelerate smoothly throughout the casting stroke. Make a conscious effort not to move your wrist; the wrist snap will come automatically at the proper time, at the completion of the arm movement.

As you make the backcast, turn and look over your right shoulder; stop at the end of this backcast stroke. Did you see the rolling loop develop and then unroll? Now take a look at where the rod is pointed. It should be pointing only 30 inches or so behind vertical (at 1:00 on the imaginary clock). If you stopped the rod at the 1 o'clock position, the line will have traveled in an upward direction from the rod tip and unrolled well above the ground. Repeat this exercise a few times, remembering to watch the line as it travels behind you.

Up to this point you have allowed the line to unroll behind you and fall to the ground. Now let's see if you can complete the cast by adding the forward cast.

Make another backcast just as you have been doing (remember to look at the backcast), and just as the tip of the line enters the rolling loop, move the reel forward quickly and smoothly by straightening out your arm in front of you. Don't allow any wrist movement until your arm demands it. This forward stroke should be a smoothly accelerating movement. See how the line moves forward now in a forward loop? Hey, you just made your first cast.

Practice the backcast followed by a forward cast until it feels natural. Remember to watch over your shoulder on every backcast because the simple act of looking back there will solve two of the most difficult problems that the beginner experiences: rod position and timing. If, when you look back, you don't see the rod, you have overrotated your wrist and lowered the rod tip out of your field of vision. The rod tip is way too low; it should have stopped at 1 o'clock, remember? Also, by looking back at the rolling loop, you don't have to guess when to start the forward cast.

On each forward cast, stop the rod high enough so that the line unrolls completely at about eye height. The line must completely unroll in the air; otherwise you're going to create a horrible disturbance on the surface of the water

as the line unrolls across it. Stop the rod at the 11 o'clock position, allow the line to unroll, and then lower the rod tip with the line as it falls to the ground.

Practice these steps for the basic cast:

- Hold rod securely, but loosely.

- Strip off 20 feet of line from reel.

- Back up so that the line lies straight out in front of you.

- Stand with your feet shoulder width apart, right toe even with left heel.

- Face in the direction of the forward cast.

- Pull off enough extra line so you can hold it in your left hand with your thumb hooked in your pocket.

- Extend casting arm to its full length.

- Pull reel quickly and smoothly to shoulder.

- Don't allow any wrist movement until your arm demands it. Stop rod movement when it reaches the 1 o'clock position.

- Look over your shoulder.

- When tip of line enters the loop, begin forward cast.

- Move reel forward quickly and smoothly by straightening arm.

- Don't allow any wrist movement until your arm demands it.

- Stop rod at the 11 o'clock position.

- Let the line unroll and then drop the rod tip with the line as it falls to the ground.

Practice, practice, practice until the sequence of movement becomes automatic and natural. Then you'll be well on your way to becoming a good fly caster.

FALSE CASTING

Up to this point, you have allowed the line to drop to the ground at the completion of the forward cast; now let's see if you can keep it in the air. This is called false casting.

Begin just as before with a backcast followed by a forward cast. At the completion of the forward cast, however, don't lower the rod top as the line unrolls. Instead, watch when the tip of the line enters the rolling loop and start another backcast by dropping your elbow and pulling the reel back near your shoulder. Don't jerk! The beginning of each casting stroke needs to be a smooth, accelerated hand movement until the wrist snaps at the end.

Right now is when you are most likely to forget to watch the backcast. If you don't turn and look each time, I can promise that you'll start having problems, so make sure you look every time.

Practice these steps for the false casting:

- Hold rod securely, but loosely.

- Strip off 20 feet of line from reel.

- Back up so that the line lies straight out in front of you.

- Stand with your feet shoulder width apart, right toe even with left heel.

- Face in the direction of the forward cast.

- Pull off enough extra line so you can hold it in your left hand with your thumb hooked in your pocket.

- Extend casting arm to its full length.

- Pull reel quickly and smoothly to shoulder.

- Don't allow any wrist movement until your arm demands it.

- Stop rod movement when it reaches the 1 o'clock position.

- Look over your shoulder.

- When tip of line enters the loop, begin forward cast.

- Move reel forward quickly and smoothly by straightening arm.

- Don't allow any wrist movement until the arm demands it.

- Stop rod at the 11 o'clock position.

- Let the line unroll. As the tip of the line enters the loop, begin backcast by quickly and smoothly pulling reel towards shoulder. Don't allow any wrist movement until the arm demands it.

- Stop backcast with the rod at the 1 o'clock position.

- Repeat steps to continue false casting.

Practice this false casting until you've really got it down. If you have gotten this far in your first session you are either an exceptionally fast learner, blessed with a lot of natural ability, or awfully tired by now. Take a break and then come back and practice some more. This is the basic casting stroke, and it must be practiced until it comes naturally.

3-12. The single-haul.

CASTING WITH BOTH HANDS

Your left hand has just been lounging around in your pocket until now, but it has a couple of important tasks to perform, so let's wake it up and start educating it.

The reason I told you to hold the line in your left hand, with your hand in your pocket, was to ensure that there was no slack line between the reel and the first guide on the rod. If you have a long loop of line hanging between the reel and the first guide, you will use most of your casting stroke to pull out that slack before you can start moving the line. Try it! Hook the line under the first finger of your rod hand and then pull some

line back through the guides until you have a loop hanging under the rod. Now, start a backcast. See how the line won't start moving until all that slack is pulled out of the loop? Well, keeping the slack out of the line is one of the jobs of the left hand.

The left hand movement is kind of tricky to learn because it is a foreign movement to most of us. The left hand moves in the opposite direction from that of the rod hand.

Let's start a casting sequence using both hands now. Extend the rod arm fully, just as you've been doing to start the casting stroke, but reach up with the left hand and grab the line just behind the first guide. Now, as you make your

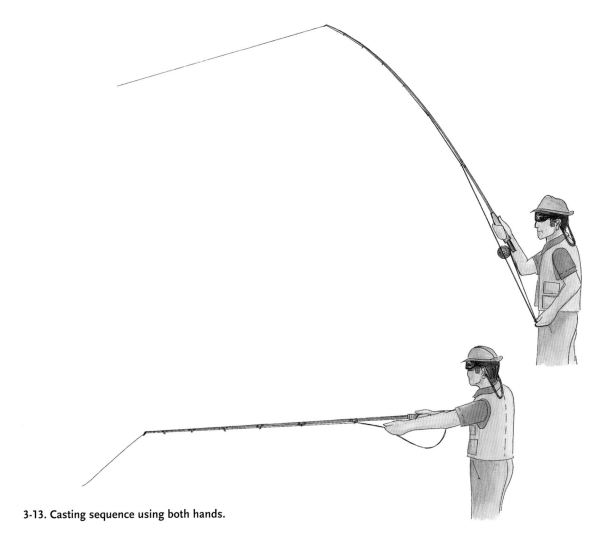

3-13. Casting sequence using both hands.

backcast motion with the right hand, pull the left hand down to your left pocket (Illus. 3-12). The first thing you should notice is that the line shoots off the ground much faster than before. This is because you are pulling the line into the rod at the same time that you are pulling the rod away from the line, creating a bow and flexing the rod considerably more than it has been. You are also making sure that none of the casting stroke is being used to simply take out any slack in the line, since you are tightening the line during the whole process. This, by the way, is called a single-haul.

That's what the left hand does on the backcast. On the forward cast, the left hand comes forward again to its original position near the first guide on the rod (Illus. 3-13). As you are false casting, move your hands away from each other during the backcast and then back together again at the completion of each forward cast, sort of like exaggerated clapping.

Another function of the left hand is to control the length of the line. To increase the length of the line that you are casting, you have to make the left hand do the work.

As you start the backcast, pull line from the reel with the left hand (an easy feat since the hands are moving apart). At the completion of the backcast, then, you will have a loop of line

3-14. Shooting line.

hanging between the left hand and the reel (Illus. 3-14). Just as you make the wrist snap at the end of the forward cast, release the line in your left hand, and the weight of the unrolling line will pull out the extra line that you pulled from the reel. This is called shooting the line.

You can continue to pull line from the reel during each backcast and shoot it during the forward cast until you have the necessary amount of line in the air. This is, in fact, how to start casting each time. Simply shake out a few feet of line on the water and then start false casting, adding line during each forward cast, until you have the desired amount of line working.

By shortening the amount of line in the air while false casting, you can reverse the process. During each backcast, pull some line back in by rolling it through the left hand and letting it fall in a loop between your hand and the reel.

This ability to change line length during the casting stroke is one of the main purposes for false casting. While false casting, you can see how long the line is as it unrolls during each forward cast. Then you can adjust its length so that the fly will land where desired.

When false casting you can move around in the stream without reeling in all of the line each time you move and without having to drag it along on the water. This cast is also good for drying the fly.

REVIEW OF THE BASIC CASTING STROKE

Let's review the main points of the basic casting stroke:

- Hold rod securely, but loosely.

- Strip off 10 feet of line from reel.

- Stand with your feet shoulder width apart, right toe even with left heel.

- Face in the direction of the forward cast.

- Pull off enough extra line so you can hold it in your left hand while extending the casting arm to its full length.

- Pull reel quickly and smoothly to shoulder as left hand pulls extra line from the reel and drops to your side. Don't allow any wrist movement in the rod hand until the arm demands it.

- Stop rod movement with the rod at the 1 o'clock position.

- Look over your shoulder.

- When tip of line enters the loop, begin forward cast.

- Move reel forward quickly and smoothly by straightening out your arm.

- Don't allow any wrist movement until your arm demands it.

- Stop rod at the 11 o'clock position.

- As the line unrolls, release the extra line held in your left hand. As the tip of the line enters the loop, begin backcast by quickly and smoothly pulling reel towards your shoulder. Don't allow any wrist movement until your arm demands it.

- Stop backcast with the rod at the 1 o'clock position.

- Repeat steps to continue false casting, adding line at the completion of each forward cast until desired line length is reached.

The toughest of these to control are stopping the rod at the right position, timing when to start the rod moving in the opposite direction, and not overrotating the wrist. All of these problems can be solved very easily by just looking over your shoulder as you complete each backcast: you can check rod position (stopping at the right point and not overrotating the wrist) and see when to start the forward cast. I can't emphasize enough the importance of looking at the backcast. It will solve all of the really tough problems of fly casting.

LOOP CONTROL

One of the built-in advantages of this casting method is that you can achieve a good cast with a tight loop. What in the world is a tight loop, you say? Well, what we are talking about is the shape of the rolling loop that develops during the cast. If the space between the top and bottom sections of the fly line is narrow, we say that we have a tight loop. If there is a large space between the two sections of line, we call that a wide loop. Does it really matter? You bet it does!

A tight loop is much more efficient for moving the line through the air, for a number of reasons. The tight loop presents less frontal area to the air mass and, thus, is subject to less friction. This becomes critical when casting into a stout wind. Since there is less distance between the two parts of the line, there is less tendency for the loop to get blown over into a horizontal instead of a vertical position by a wind from the side. Because there is less frontal area, the loop penetrates the wind better. But, most important, a tight loop develops greater line speed for us. By decreasing the radius of the curve that the line is passing through, the line is forced to travel faster. And the faster the line unrolls, the less time gravity has to pull it to the ground.

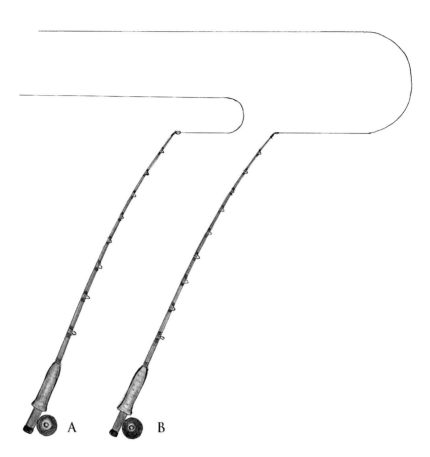

3-15. A. Tight loop. B. A wide loop. A B

The casting method that you have been practicing was designed specifically to produce a good, tight loop, and it is important that you understand just what controls the width of the loop. But in order to explain how to throw a tight loop, we have to explain first how to throw a wide one.

If, as you complete the forward cast, you drop the rod tip below the 1 o'clock position, then you are actually moving the lower section of line down and away from the upper section, forming a wide loop. If, on the other hand, you keep the rod tip up so that its movement forms a line parallel to the ground, then you are keeping the two parts of the line very close together, forming a very tight loop. See Illus. 3-15A and B for pictures of these situations. It can, however, be too tight, because if the rod were actually moving in a line perfectly parallel to the ground, the line would hit the rod. The wrist snap at each end of the

casting stroke and the subsequent lowering of the rod tip keep that from happening, because they enable the line to clear the rod.

Although there are some real advantages to a tight loop and that is certainly the basic cast that you need to develop, sometimes your might need to cast a wide loop, as you would when presenting a dry fly. If you cast a nice tight loop for your presentation, the line will be traveling so fast it will cause the leader to unroll with too much force, and the fly will land too hard on the water. You can avoid this by driving the forward cast out as usual, and when you snap your wrist, raise your elbow away from your side. This will enable you to drop the rod tip lower than usual and will open up the loop, slow down its unrolling, and make a quieter presentation on the water (Illus. 3-16). Another time when you might want to throw a wide loop is when you use weighted flies that drop faster than the fly line. With a

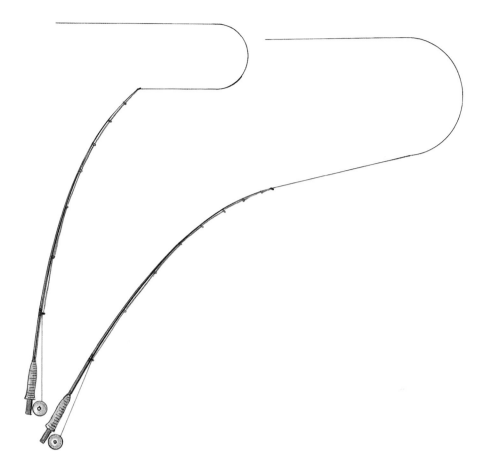

3-16. Lowering the rod tip.

tight loop, the fly might snag on the lower section of the loop, while a wide loop would prevent the problem. In practice, fly fishers constantly change their casting strokes to adjust loop size. To cast a longer line, you must tighten up the loop to increase line speed. This acceleration is required so the line will still unroll completely while it's well above the ground. A wind from your back will require a cast in which you open up the loop a little to decrease line speed, since the wind is helping the line unroll faster. If casting a dry fly to a smooth, still section of water, you will really open up the loop. The leader will then turn the fly over well above the water so it can drop softly to the surface. These adjustments are made subconsciously and only after a lot of actual fishing.

But the tight loop is the bread and butter cast of the fly fisher, so be sure you practice the basic casting stroke until it comes automatically.

Then start working on the necessary variations. And don't spend too many hours practicing on grass, either; it can actually prolong the learning process. Why? Because you think too much!

My recommendation is to practice until you have the basic cast down fairly well and then head for the river. When you're out actually trying to present the fly to the trout, your conscious mind is busy making all sorts of judgments in choosing a fly pattern, in reading the water, and in making the presentation, which leaves your subconscious mind to handle the casting side of things. It's amazing how well your subconscious can solve casting problems if it isn't interrupted all the time. While you're on the stream you will also discover that the nice straight cast that you just learned won't always put the fly where you need it. There are several other casts that you should know in order to be an effective fly fisher.

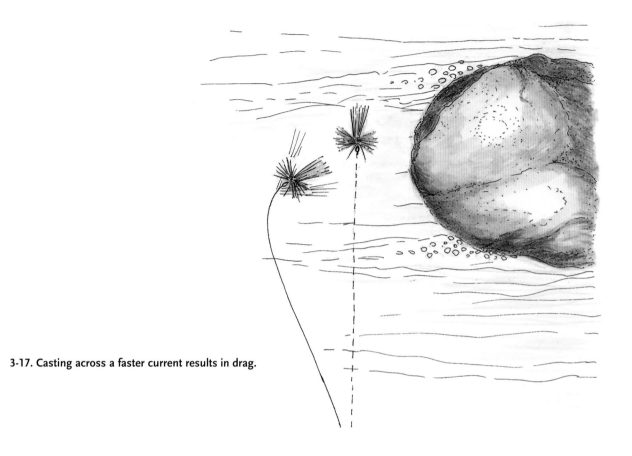

3-17. Casting across a faster current results in drag.

Other Casts

REACH CAST

This cast is used as a tool to counter drag. Let's say you want to cast to a spot on the other side of a section of faster current that is moving from your right to your left. If you were to cast in a straight line directly across the stream, the faster current between you and the fly would create a downstream belly in the line and pull the fly back towards you (Illus. 3-17). This movement of the fly in a direction other than a natural drift with the current is what we call drag, and trout won't normally take a dragging fly. With the reach cast you can make the line land upstream from the fly. There the fly is free to drift naturally until the faster current pulls the belly of the line down below the fly. These few feet of natural drift enable you to present the fly without drag.

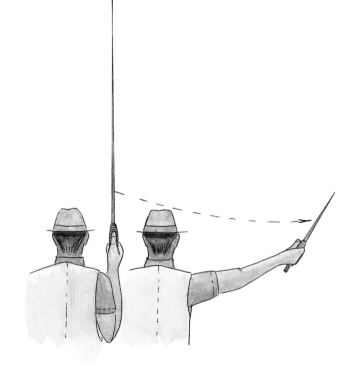

3-18. The reach cast.

3-19. The curve cast.

The reach cast is made by aiming the cast at a point where you want to begin the natural drift. As the final forward cast (called the presentation cast) is straightening out, move the rod upstream (Illus. 3-18). This upstream movement of the rod ensures that the line will fall on the water upstream of the fly's position and provide a few feet of drag-free drift. The reach cast is useful and pretty easy to master, so be sure to include it in your practice sessions.

CURVE CAST

This cast can serve the same purpose as the reach cast; the fly lands downstream from the line when casting across stream. It also has other uses. At the completion of a curve cast, the last 8 to 10 feet of line and the leader form a curve (Illus. 3-19). This curve in the end of the line and leader enables the cast to go around to the other side of an obstacle, such as a rock. The curve cast isn't easy to master, and most of us can only make a good curve cast in one direction: a left curve if you are right-handed or a right curve if you are left-handed.

To make a curve cast, rotate your arm to the right (for a right-handed caster) from the elbow (Illus. 3-20), as you complete the presentation cast. Rotate your arm just prior to the wrist snap at the end of the casting stroke. What you are doing is flexing the rod in a rear arc as you load it during the start of the casting stroke, just as in a

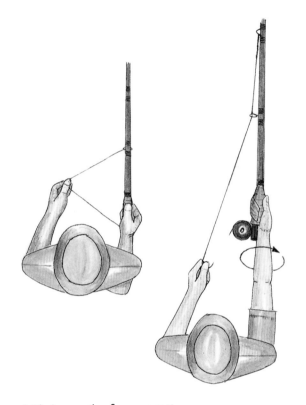

3-20. Arm motion for curve cast.

normal forward cast. Then at the end of the cast, rolling your arm changes the direction in which the rod throws the line. The line will go out in the direction of the casting stroke; but towards the end of the cast, the rolling loop will lie down horizontally. Now the line is unrolling from right to left around the horizontal loop, and as it finishes unrolling, the end of the line and leader will snap around to the left of the main portion of the line.

It will take some time for the line, the leader, and the fly to snap around and form the curve; so you must aim the cast a little higher above the water than normal and add a little additional force to the cast. Otherwise the line will land on the water before the curve is formed.

The rolling of the wrist is what makes the curve cast work. It is very difficult for a right-handed caster to roll the wrist strongly and quickly in a counterclockwise rotation to make the line curve to the right. There are a lot of fly casters who can throw a curve cast equally well in either direction, but it really takes long, hard practice.

My right curve is about 50% as effective as my left curve. The reach cast is just as effective as the curve cast for getting a drag-free drift across

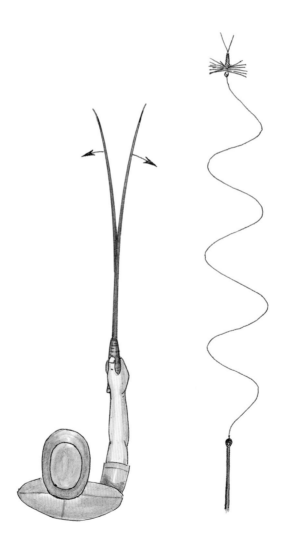

3-21. The S-cast.

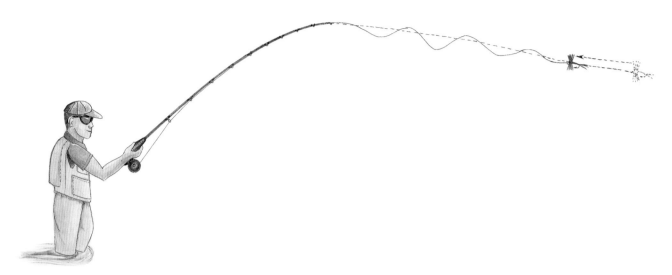

3-22. The stop cast.

the current, and it's a lot easier to do. But when you need to get the fly into a pocket on the other side of an obstruction, the curve cast is what you need. It isn't easy to develop but will be well worth practicing.

S-CAST

This is also called a serpentine or snake cast. The purpose of the S-cast is to put additional line on the water in the form of S's (Illus. 3-21) so that the fly can travel downstream for some distance without drag. It is a very easy cast to make. Make your normal forward cast but aim it a little higher than usual above the water. When the line unrolls, shake the rod tip gently from side to side as the line drops towards the water. This will throw a series of waves in the line, and your fly can drift downstream drag-free until all of the curves are out of the line. This cast is used for fishing downstream or slightly across and down. While false casting, keep in mind that you will need to cast a longer line than normal if the fly is to land at the desired spot, since

the curves in the line will shorten its span across the water.

STOP CAST

The stop cast achieves the same effect as the S-cast; it puts extra line on the water to avoid drag when casting downstream, or down and across the stream. To make the stop cast, simply add some additional power to your normal forward cast (again, aim slightly higher above the water) and then stop the rod suddenly at the completion of the cast (Illus. 3-22).

The sudden stop will cause the line to "bounce" back towards you and lay extra slack on the water. Like the S-cast, the stop cast requires adding extra line to your cast to allow for the slack when the fly lands on the water. The stop cast is just as effective as the S-cast but a little more difficult to execute. Using either of them makes it difficult to control the exact landing position of the fly, but if you are casting across a faster or slower current, or fishing downstream, you simply must be able to get that extra slack on the water.

ROLL CAST

The roll cast is used when obstructions behind you prevent your making a normal backcast. In the roll cast, the line will never pass behind you. The roll cast is started with the line on the water. You begin by lifting the rod tip as you pull slack in with the line hand. The line, leader, and fly will start sliding towards you on the surface of the water. Continue to lift the rod tip smoothly as you pull the rod back to the 11 o'clock position. Slowly and smoothly, remember. When the rod reaches the 11 o'clock position, move it forward and down quickly and strongly. The tip of the line will continue to move towards you and then come up off the water into a forward rolling loop (Illus. 3-23). You'll have to wait to practice the roll cast until you can get to some water. It just won't work off grass because grass doesn't have as much resistance-causing friction as water does and won't load the rod.

As I said, the main purpose for a roll cast is to avoid having to make a backcast, but it also works well in situations where you want to make repeated short casts, particularly when fishing nymphs or streamers where you don't need to false-cast to dry the fly.

The roll cast can also be used to pick up the fly from the water and is especially useful when casting upstream. In this situation, the fly comes back downstream towards you, and it is sometimes very difficult to strip in line fast enough to keep the slack out. If you try to start the pickup of the line with slack on the water, your rod movement will only serve to take the slack out of the line and won't pick up the line. If you start a quick roll cast, though, you can immediately get

3-23. The roll cast.

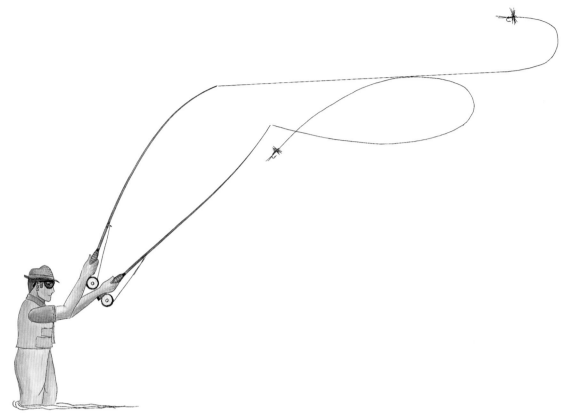

3-24. The roll-cast pickup.

the line up off the water into a forward rolling loop (Illus. 3-24). But don't let it unroll completely. As the forward loop unrolls, immediately go into a normal backcast.

This roll-cast pickup is indispensable during the great caddis hatch on the Arkansas River each spring, when we do a lot of upstream dry fly-fishing.

DOUBLE-HAUL

The ability to cast the double-haul has, for some unknown reason, always been the litmus test of a good fly caster. Well, it just ain't so! Like all of the other special casts, the double-haul was designed to perform a specific job—to enable us to cast a

longer line. It isn't any more difficult to understand or learn than, say, the curve cast, and it's not nearly as useful either.

In the basic casting stroke, the single-haul is the movement of the line hand away from the rod during the pickup. The double-haul is simply a matter of adding that same kind of movement at the start of the forward cast. The big difference is that the line hand isn't near the first guide on the rod at the completion of the backcast, so we need to get it up there.

To make a double-haul, you first strip off several feet of line so that there is a large loop of slack between the reel and your line hand. Then start a normal backcast, pulling the rod back to

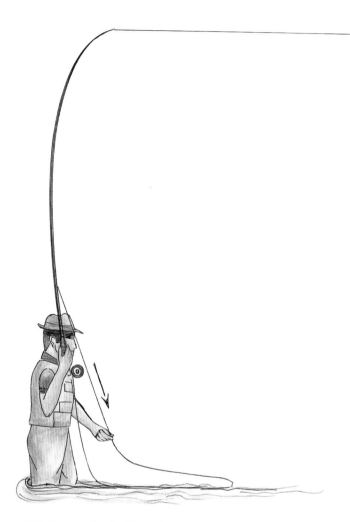

3-25. Starting the double-haul.

the 1 o'clock position with the rod hand while the line hand moves quickly to your hip (Illus. 3-25). As soon as the rod stops at the backcast position, drift your left hand across your body (the unrolling line will pull out the line as you feed it into the guide) until it comes close to the first guide (Illus. 3-26). At this point, your left hand is across your body, reaching up towards the first guide on the rod.

Now start the forward cast by pulling quickly and firmly on the line with your left hand, at the same time that you start the rod forward (Illus. 3-27). This pulling of the line into the rod

will establish more flex than normal and store more potential energy in the rod. At the completion of the forward rod movement, release the extra line between your line hand and the reel so it can be pulled out through the guides (Illus. 3-28).

Normally, the double-haul is used only where you need extra power to unroll a long cast. But occasionally (when casting into a strong wind, for instance) you will need to get a lot of power into the cast, and the double-haul will do it for you.

The trick to learning the double-haul is to start off with a very short line-hand movement.

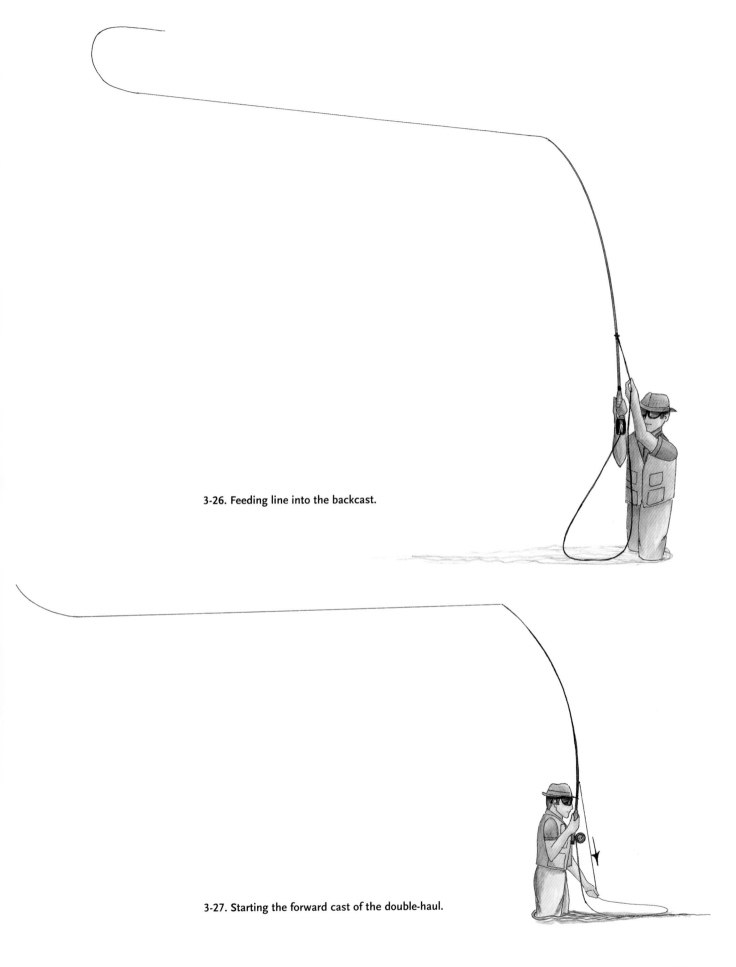

3-26. Feeding line into the backcast.

3-27. Starting the forward cast of the double-haul.

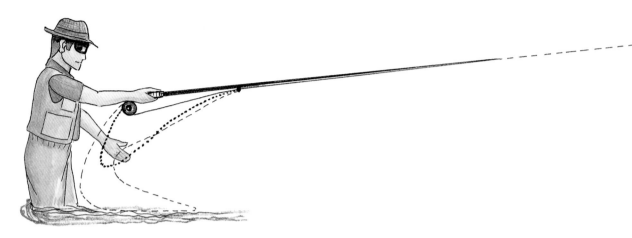

3-28. Release (shoot) the slack line during the double-haul.

At the completion of the backcast don't try to reach up to the rod; just move your line hand 6 inches or so in that direction, wait for the backcast to unroll, and then pull down as you make the forward cast. Once you get the timing right you can start increasing the length of the reach towards the rod. It won't take too long until you reach clear up across your body and pull all the way back down to your hip.

One more thing that should be said about casting: a good fly fisher never casts more line than necessary. It takes too much work. A long line is much harder to control both in the air and on the water, and the difficulty in hooking a fish is almost in direct proportion to the length of the line being used. It's a rare day on the trout stream when you don't see someone overly pleased at how far they can cast, and their fishing suffers for it. Sometimes we simply can't get into a better casting position by wading closer and are forced to make a long cast. But those times are pretty rare. A shorter line catches more fish!

You will discover numerous other casting techniques for getting the fly where it needs to be so that it can drift properly without drag. The ones we have covered are the basics, and you will soon discover that in a day's fishing you will use each of them and probably some of your own. Don't be afraid to experiment. Getting the fly to the fish is the name of the game, and if it takes an innovative, improvised technique to get it there—and it works—you're to be congratulated.

Having Problems?

To spare you the trouble of searching through the entire chapter for the solution to a particular casting problem, we are including a section on what could go wrong and how to correct it.

Cracking line: If you hear a loud crack as you start the forward cast, or if you are snapping off flies, you are starting the forward cast too soon. To solve the problem, look over your shoulder at the

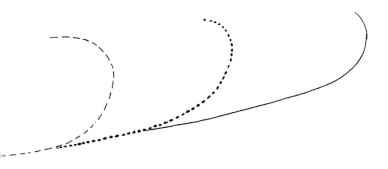

backcast and start the forward cast just as the tip of the line enters the rolling loop.

Backcast too low: This problem can be caused by waiting too long for the line to straighten, by allowing it to fall too low behind you, or by allowing the rod to drift back and down too far at the completion of the backcast. The most common cause is letting your wrist flex too far at the completion of the backcast: the rod must not go back farther than the 1 o'clock position. The other possibility is that you are waiting too long before starting the forward cast. Both problems can be corrected by looking over your shoulder at the completion of the backcast. If you can't see the rod tip, you are flexing your wrist too much and bringing the rod too low; you should start the forward cast as the tip of the line enters the rolling loop.

Wide loop: If your casting loop is too wide, it is probably because you are using too much wrist in the cast. Another possible cause of throwing a

wide loop is that you are moving the rod up in an arc during the forward cast. Remember to push the rod out and pull it back during the casting stroke. If you think in terms of moving the reel parallel to the ground, your loop will tighten up.

Tailing (or closed) loop: A tailing loop is formed when the tip of the line drops below the bottom section of the line in the casting loop; there are several possible causes. The most common one is delaying the start of the forward cast too long, which allows the line to drop below the rod tip on the backcast. Starting the forward cast with the line very far below the rod tip means that the line will form an inverted loop as it comes up and over the rod tip, resulting in the tailing loop. The solution is, once again, to look at the backcast and start forward as the tip of the line enters the rolling loop; also check rod position on the backcast. Another common cause of the tailing loop is overpowering the forward cast. By overpowering the forward cast, you make the rod flex more than normal, which lowers the line position and tightens the loop. If your backcast rod position and timing seem to be just right, try using less power during the forward cast. Attempting to throw too tight a loop will also often cause a tailing loop. Keep in mind that wind, fly weight, and tippet size will all have an effect on how tight a loop you can throw without the fly dropping below the line. If this is the problem, just open up the loop a little by lowering the rod tip a few more inches at the completion of both the back and forward casts.

Lack of power: This is usually a timing problem, most often caused by starting the forward cast too soon. If the forward cast is started too quickly, there isn't enough line straightened out to adequately flex the rod for the forward cast. Again, the solution is to look at the backcast to ensure that your timing for starting the forward cast is correct.

Line or fly hitting you or rod: This can be dangerous. A #6 streamer in the ear is not pleasant! Wind from the direction of your casting arm is often the culprit in this case, blowing the line into you and the rod. The best solution is to lower the rod tip to a plane of movement more perpendicular to the wind; that is, lower the rod tip toward a side-arm casting position. The other possible problem is that you are not moving the rod in a constant plane during both the forward and backward casts. If you move the line forward in one plane and back in another, you will establish a circular movement of the line, and you're probably standing on the edge of the circle. To solve the problem, make sure that the rod is moving on the same plane during both the forward and back casts.

Fly not turning over properly: If your fly isn't turning over correctly, there are several possible causes, but the most common is incorrect tippet size. Too light a tippet will fail to support the fly to the completion of the cast and will cause it to fall too soon. Too heavy a tippet will overpower the weight of the fly, forcing it to turn over too forcefully, and it will splash on the water. The starting point for determining tippet size is to divide the fly size by 4 and use a tippet with that X designation. In some cases (wind, bushy flies, and so on) you may need to vary from the rule of dividing by 4 to get proper turnover. Another possible problem is improper power application: either too much or too little power on the forward cast. Overpowering the forward cast causes the fly to turn over too forcefully because as the rolling loop moves into the leader, there is so much momentum remaining that the leader can't dissipate it. Underpowering the forward cast results in the leader not straightening out because all of the momentum in the rolling loop was used up before the leader straightened out.

Any beginner worth his salt will find new problems, but we have included here some of the most common ones. Intentionally being redundant, I will repeat: nearly all your casting problems can be solved simply by looking over your shoulder at the backcast.

PRESENTATION

Probably the single most important factor for success in fly-fishing is something we call presentation. By presentation we mean the entire sequence that occurs from the time the fly drops to the water until it passes the point where the feeding fish should take it. The first decision, then, is to decide just exactly where the fly should be placed on the water. This entails something fly fishers call "reading the water."

Reading the Water

Reading the water involves two basic steps: (1) determining where the fish is likely to be, and (2) figuring out where we need to cast to get the fly to drift down to the fish, while avoiding the unnatural movement of the fly, called drag.

FINDING THE FISH

If there are actively feeding fish present, it's not too tough to figure out where they are. You can see the riseforms (the water disturbances created as they take insects). If there are no obvious signs of feeding, look in places where they are likely to be. Generally, trout can be found in one of three positions in the stream: in a resting lie, a feeding lie, or a primary lie (Illus. 4-1).

The resting lie, or "bedroom," is where the trout retires when he isn't actively pursuing food. The resting lie (Illus. 4-2A through E) must be the kind of place where he doesn't have to expend a great amount of energy to hold his position and where he has adequate protection from his natural enemies.

Examples include undercut banks, beneath logs and rocks, or in deep, slow-moving pools.

▥ 4-1. TYPES OF LIES.

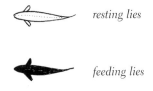 *resting lies*

feeding lies

 *primary lies*

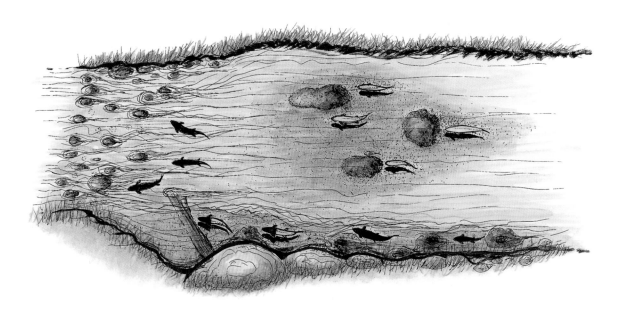

■ 4-2 A–E. RESTING LIES.

A

B

C

D

E

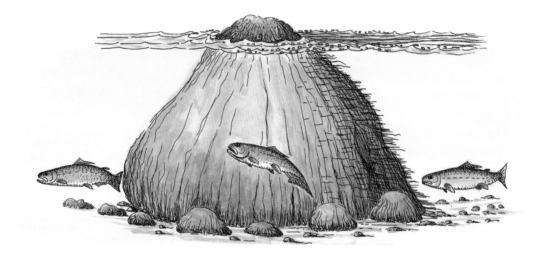

The feeding lie (Illus. 4-3A through C) is the trout's workplace. Ideally, it is located where a lot of food is available, where he doesn't have to work too hard to stay in position, and where he is protected. Feeding lies are nearly always on edges. Let me repeat that because it may be the most important point in this whole book. Feeding lies are nearly always on edges! Edges of what? Any edges—the edge along a rock, a shore, a log, and most important, the edges between fast and slow water. The reason that these are such good feeding lies is that food, carried along by the natural motion of the water, gathers there. Additionally, since it is the edge of something, there is quiet water immediately adjacent in which the trout can hold its position with a minimum expenditure of energy and still be able to feed readily. Note that the boundary between the water and the stream bottom is also an edge.

A

B

C

A

B

A primary lie is one where the fish has it all—breakfast in bed. It is an area where a lot of food is easily obtainable and which affords constant protection (Illus. 4-4A and B). Although primary lies in any one section of stream are rare, you should learn to recognize them because they harbor the biggest trout. Like the bully at the movies, he chases everyone smaller out of the choicest spot. Primary lies are always near edges where food gathers, but they differ from plain old feeding lies because water movement is at a minimum near these edges, and the cover affords protection. The back corner of an undercut rock is often a primary lie, an undercut bank where the current makes a turn out of a small pocket and forms a food-catching eddy is a good spot, and a partially submerged log where the current bangs up against it and then turns and runs parallel to it is another. These primary lies aren't abundant in any stream, but, then again, neither are the really large fish that they often hold.

Casting Position

Being able to recognize areas where the trout can most likely be found is one of the prerequisites for the successful fly fisher, but it is only the first step in hooking the fish. We have to be able to get the fly to the proper point so that it comes to the fish in a natural manner; it must appear to be just another piece of food.

The dry fly and nymph fishermen have to work constantly to overcome the effects of current-induced drag on the fly so that it will appear to the trout as a natural insect would. This ability to handle the fly, leader, and line on or in the water to avoid drag is one of the most difficult aspects of fly-fishing.

For the most part, a dry fly must drift downstream as if there were no leader attached. It must move evenly with the surrounding current. Any movement of the fly other than what is natural to that particular current is drag. A fly that moves more slowly than the surrounding current drags and a fly that moves sideways, or across the current, also drags.

Drag in which the fly moves across the current is the most common. This across-current drag is caused by the line or leader passing across a current that is moving at a different speed from the section of water that the fly is in. If the current between the angler and the fly is faster than the speed of the water where the fly is, the faster current will take the line downstream faster than the fly is moving, until all the slack between the line and fly is removed. At that point, the fly will start moving laterally across the stream, curving back towards the angler (Illus. 4-5).

4-5. Drag resulting from casting across a faster current.

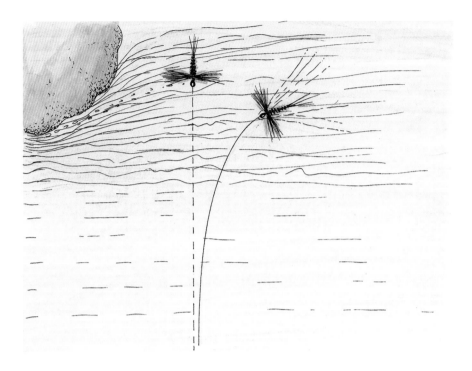

4-6. Drag resulting from casting across a slower current.

An intervening current that is slower than that where the fly is floating will produce a similar result. As soon as the slack is taken from the leader, the fly will be pulled in an upstream direction, resulting in the fly moving across current, curving towards the angler (Illus. 4-6).

The reason that this is the most common type of drag situation seen by the fly fisher is very simple. First of all, it is the most common fishing situation found on the stream because we normally fish at an upstream angle across the stream, and there are nearly always several currents of varying speeds between us and the fly. Second, this lateral drag, with the fly moving back towards us, is recognized because the fly often leaves a wake across the surface and is quickly pulled under the surface of the water.

The difficulty, though, is that the drag is often so subtle that we can't see it from our casting position. Even an inch or two of unnatural lateral movement of the fly is enough to keep the trout from being fooled by our offering, and, from

our casting position 30 or 40 feet away, we simply can't detect that small, unnatural movement of the fly.

This problem really came to my attention a few years ago while fishing the upper meadow section of the Gibbon in Yellowstone with Bob Damico. The river is beautiful in that area. We had been taking trout successfully on grasshopper patterns, which we floated into the feeding lies in each of the bends. I had watched as Bob made two or three drifts through one of the bends without getting a take, and it just seemed to me that that particular spot had to hold a large trout. It was a classic primary lie. Sure enough, within a couple of minutes after he had moved on I saw a quiet swirl behind the rock in the corner of the bend, precisely where Bob's fly had drifted. I watched the bend out of the corner of my eye as I fished my way towards it and saw the same fish rise three or four more times.

I cautiously moved up to a good casting position and laid the line across the pool so that the fly landed 6 or 8 feet above the riseforms and held my breath as the fly came over the fish—no take. I allowed the fly to swing well below the trout, and as I picked up the line to start my backcast, he rose again! Again, I drifted the fly over the feeding spot without a take, and just as before, he rose to take a natural as I was making my backcast.

Aha, I thought, he's feeding in a rhythm and I'm out of sync with his feeding cycle. I false-cast a few times to delay my presentation so my fly would arrive a few seconds later, and he rose to a natural before my fly got to him! I put on a fresh fly. I cast more quickly. I cast more slowly. And finally, in the throes of exasperation, I made a sloppy cast and he quit rising.

Bob was waiting for me a few bends away, and when I told him about the experience, he volunteered to cross the river to the trout's side and see if he could determine the problem. I moved back down into the casting position as Bob crawled up close to the feeding lie. We watched a few minutes and saw that the fish had started feeding again. I made the same presentation that I had used before, again without success. After I cast three or four times with no result, Bob moved quietly to the upper end of the bend where he could look straight downstream. When I made the next drift, he noticed that the leader was catching on a narrow tongue of fast water and making a quick sideways movement of a couple of inches just at the spot where the trout was taking the fly.

I extended my cast a foot or so and made a sudden stop at the end of the cast, so that the fly flipped back to the leader to get a little more slack near the fly and extend the drag-free drift. On the second cast the trout sucked the fly in without hesitation. It would be nice to say that it was a

huge 4-pound trout and relate the ensuing battle. In reality, though, it was a nice, scrappy 14-inch brown, which was a bit of an anticlimax to all the work we had gone through to take him. It was a lesson well learned, however, and taught me that when you can't induce the trout to the fly, it's often the presentation that's causing the problem.

Now, before changing from a fly that has been working or going to a finer tippet, I try several different presentations from several different casting positions to avoid unseen drag. Often, just moving a couple of feet one way or the other before making the cast results in a more natural drift that will fool a finicky feeder.

Keep in mind that you must present the fly to the trout in his feeding lie, not where you see the riseform. Vince Marinaro, in his book *In the Ring of the Rise*, shows beautiful photographs of feeding trout that, without exception, actually take the food several feet downstream from where they watch for food. The fish remains in position until he sees the food approach and then he starts drifting backwards in the current, tipping up, until the fly is directly overhead. At this point, he tips up until his nose is just under the surface; with a quick pump of the gills he pulls the fly into his mouth. He then drops down and swims back upstream to his feeding lie.

If you were to cast your fly to where the riseform was seen, you would be casting behind the trout, and he probably wouldn't even see it. To present your fly to the trout, then, you need to land it 4 to 6 feet above where you see the riseform. By the way, *In the Ring of the Rise* is one of the most delightful books for the angler and should be on your required reading list. It not only contains the beautiful and important photographs of feeding trout, but it also presents a lot of information on feeding trout that will serve you well.

Defeating Drag

The fly fisher employs many tricks to defeat drag. By far the most common presentation is the "across and up." The fly is cast to a fish that is lying somewhere between straight across stream and a point about 60 degrees or so upstream. The fly is, as always, cast to a point 4 to 6 feet above the spot where the fish is taking food from the surface (Illus. 4-7).

We often use an S-cast, curve cast, or reach cast so that the fly arrives at the trout's position before the force of the current on the line and leader can cause the fly to drag. Remember, always cast so that the fly lands well above the riseforms. If the fly isn't taken, be sure to let it drift well past the fish before starting the backcast so that the disturbance caused by the pickup doesn't disturb the trout.

Instead of casting so far across the stream, with all the currents between you and the fly, we sometimes move towards the middle of the stream, so that the line runs more parallel to the stream flow and is affected by fewer currents of different speeds. But don't cast straight upstream, or the line will drift across the fish before the fly gets there (called "lining" the fish), and you'll spook the trout. The other problem with a sharp upstream presentation is that the line moves back towards you very fast, and if you can't strip the line in quickly enough, there will be so much slack on the water that you can't set the hook when the fish does take (Illus. 4-8).

Floating the fly downstream to the fish is another method that is often successful in getting the drag-free fly to the trout's position. This, however, is probably the most difficult presentation to make. Drag is thwarted because the fly is

4-7. "Across and up" presentation.

already moving ahead of the line and leader, and all three are in the same current, moving at the same speed. Controlling the slack is the problem here. If there isn't enough slack in the line and leader, the fly will be stopped by the straightened-out line and leader before it gets to the fish. Too much slack (Illus. 4-9) means that there is still slack in the leader and line when the trout takes, and you can't impart any force to the fly to set the hook.

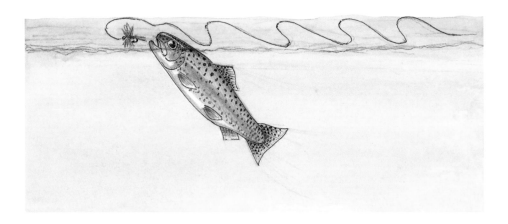

4-8. Too much slack to set the hook.

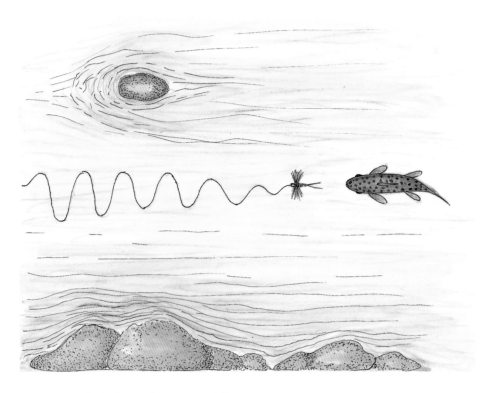

4-9. Too much slack on a downstream drift.

The setting of the hook is, in itself, a problem with the downstream presentation (Illus. 4-10). The fly is drifting down to the fish, and when he does take it and you set the hook, you are pulling the fly back upstream—out of his mouth!

Generally, you must wait for the trout to drop back down from the surface before applying any movement to set the hook. This way, the hook moves slightly up towards the surface and will set in the upper lip of the trout. This downstream presentation is tricky business, but one which is invaluable to the fly fisher. You will undoubtedly miss more fish fishing downstream than with any other method. But to paraphrase an old lover's lament, "'tis better to have missed the take, than never to have had the take at all."

With practice, you learn to judge just how much line to put on the water so that nearly all the slack will be used up by the time the fly gets to the fish, and your timing for setting the hook becomes well honed. After eliminating these two problems, you will find this to be a very effective method of presenting a fly to a feeding trout in difficult currents.

The problem of getting a drag-free presentation of a nymph is compounded by a couple of things. The obvious is that you can't see the fly and the currents' effect on it. Second, the nymph is being fished underwater, where the added dimension of vertical movement is present. Not only is the fly subjected to lateral drag, it may also be bounced up and down in the flow. If this vertical movement of the artificial matches that of the naturals in the water, there is no problem. But a weighted nymph might be detected as being foreign by the trout because it didn't bounce in the right spot, just as readily as if it displayed an unnatural lateral movement. The only real solution to getting a natural presentation with a

4-10. Not enough slack on a downstream drift.

nymph is trial and error; and the only way you will know when you are getting the right drift will be when you start getting hits on your fly.

The experienced nymph fisherman has fished in so many different kinds of water that he has developed a sixth sense for where to cast, so that the fly is presented to the fish in a natural manner. Where to cast is an even tougher decision when fishing nymphs than when using dry flies. Not only do you have to determine where to cast to avoid drag, but you have to determine how far above the fish to place the fly for it to have time to sink to the correct depth when it passes the feeding lie. It's that extra dimension of depth that the dry-fly angler doesn't have to be concerned with.

The underwater stages of the aquatic insects are generally more active than the adult stages. Therefore, a dead, drag-free drift isn't necessarily all that is needed for the fly to appear natural to the trout. Some of the techniques that we use for fishing nymphs entail imparting motion to the fly, somewhat opposite to the dead drift that we strive for when fishing dries.

There are several different nymphing techniques for presenting the fly to the fish naturally. Charles Brooks, in *Nymph Fishing for Larger Trout*, details ten major methods and then lists another half-dozen or so minor methods. Although many of these are very similar to the basic method, there are many different approaches. Certainly, most methods do affect the presentation, but there are many other reasons for choosing one method over the others besides just getting the fly to the fish.

We'll cover these methods and how they relate to fly presentation in Chapter 6.

Streamer fishing is also subject to the difficulties of getting a good presentation, although a dead drift is rarely needed or wanted. When fishing a streamer, you are attempting to represent a minnow, and minnows are rather large, animated creatures compared to aquatic insects. For the most part, when fishing streamers you want to impart some movement to the fly to imitate better the swimming, darting movement of the minnow.

Much as when fishing nymphs, the biggest problems facing the angler are that you can't see the fly and how it is behaving in the water, and you can't determine exactly where to cast so that the fly lands where it will sink to the proper depth and moves correctly when passing the trout's suspected position.

Streamer Fly Tying and Fishing by Joseph D. Bates, Jr., has been around for many years but is still the best treatment of streamer fishing. It is devoted entirely to methods and imitations for streamer fishing. He discusses almost a dozen ways of presenting the streamer to the fish, many of which closely parallel the techniques used by the nymph fisherman. Although these methods affect the presentation of the fly, there are other considerations when deciding which technique to use and why. We will cover these and other streamer techniques in more depth in Chapter 7.

Now that we have covered the basics of presentation, let's take a harder look at the techniques successful fly fishers use by working through some typical on-stream situations.

ON THE TOP

Dry-fly fishing is a paradox because it is the easiest method of fly-fishing in some respects and the most difficult in others. It is the easiest method in that the angler can see what is going on; everything happens out in the open in plain view. You can read the surface of the water more easily than you can read the area below the surface; you can watch your fly as it is presented to the trout and evaluate its performance; you can readily identify the food that is being taken; you can often tell how and where to fish because the trout has given away his position by creating a surface disturbance; and, perhaps most important, you can definitely tell when the fish takes your offering.

The difficulties arise because the trout is exposed while surface feeding and is generally more wary than when feeding beneath the surface. You simply must be able to cast well to be consistently successful in taking fish. You not only have to be able to handle the fly line well in the air, but you must be capable of controlling it on the water. Leader length and tippet size become critical factors in many cases, much more so than when fishing underwater. Despite the difficulties, we recommend that the beginner start here if local fishing conditions allow it.

The difficulties are not insurmountable. And the skills you develop while learning to fish dry flies will enable you to become a good all-round fly fisher. You could fish nymphs all your life and catch a lot of trout without ever learning to cast well, and you could fish streamers expertly without ever getting very involved with leaders or presentation. It is much easier for the dry-fly fisherman to learn to fish nymphs or streamers than the other way around, because the dry-fly fisherman has already developed the basic range of skills.

On the other hand, learning to detect the almost imperceptible strike when the trout takes a nymph is a hundred times more difficult than watching the rise to your floating fly. You must also determine just where you need to cast the streamer so that it will pass the point where you infer the trout to be. Knowing where to cast is often evident when fishing dries, since you can see the fish and his feeding spot. Fishing dries also involves one less dimension than fishing "down under"—there is no depth to the water's surface. But the most important advantage to dry-fly fishing for the beginner is that everything is laid out in front of you, and you can see when you have gotten everything just right and when you have made a mistake. Your skills, therefore, will develop faster than if you have to guess what is going on. Any time you take trout on a fly rod you are having fun. But most fly fishers, even most dyed-in-the-wool nymphers, will agree that the thrill of seeing the trout take the fly is the most fun of all.

Equipment for Dry-Fly Fishing

We certainly aren't going to advocate buying a different set of equipment for each type of fly-fishing that you do. If you can foresee spending a lot more time fishing one type than another, you might want to tailor your equipment towards that end.

RODS

It seems that most dry-fly fishermen prefer rods with a smooth, rather slow (or soft) action, and we agree. It just seems more difficult to make a gentle presentation with a powerful, fast-action rod. A popular rod length seems to be 8½ feet, although 9-foot and even 9½-foot rods are often chosen. The longer rod makes casting above the bank and its brush easier. It's easier to cast a longer line with a longer rod because the casting lever is longer, and you have a greater backcast height built into the rod. The extra reach that the longer rod provides makes it much easier to mend and control the line on the water, too.

All other things being equal, most dry-fly fishermen seem to choose a rod that casts a lighter line than they would use for nymph or streamer fishing. Their feeling is that the lighter line creates less surface disturbance—a hard argument to dispute. But you must consider the casting conditions that you will commonly face. If you are often confronted with wind, it doesn't make sense to choose a smaller line size, which will make casting and presentation more difficult. If you have to make two or three casts to get the fly where it needs to be, you certainly haven't made less surface disturbance! Probably the best recommendation is to use the lightest line that allows you to cast comfortably, because when fishing dry flies, you are going to be doing a lot more casting. This casting is going to be much more critical than when fishing nymphs or streamers.

LEADERS AND TIPPETS

Leader selection is extremely important when fishing dry flies because your presentation of the fly is dependent upon the leader unrolling properly at the completion of the cast. You'll remember that in Chapter 1 we mentioned the Rule of

Four (divide the size of the fly by 4 to determine the tippet size for your leader). The rule works very well most of the time, but now we must qualify it a little. The rule says that if I am fishing a #12 fly, I want a 3X tippet (12 divided by 4 = 3), but what if I am using a very bushy hair-wing fly and casting into the wind? Obviously, if the 3X tippet works with a normal, sparsely hackled dry fly on a calm day, it isn't going to have enough punch to unroll a bushy fly on a windy day. The number of variables that the fly fisher, and particularly the dry-fly fisherman, is faced with precludes the use of absolute rules. The Rule of Four, like all other attempts at definitive statements, just won't hold up day in and day out on the stream. It is a good starting place and should be used as such, but if you add plain old common sense to an unusual situation, you will always (well, almost always) produce the correct answer. So, if you're using a hair-wing #12 and the leader simply won't unroll, cut the tippet back to 2X and try that. Maybe the Rule of Four isn't really a rule. Perhaps it should be called a Guideline of Four, but that doesn't sound very good, does it?

One argument you might hear for going to a very fine tippet is that there is less chance for the trout to see it. We, along with many others, just don't put much stock in that idea. We're convinced that the leader is almost always visible to the trout, just as the hook sticking out the rear of our fly is visible, but the trout's feeding instinct simply doesn't allow him to see it. Anglers must often use a smaller than normal tippet when the water is very smooth and slow moving, which would lead one to believe that the trout can see the larger leader and, therefore, refuses the fly. Those smooth, slow-moving water conditions,

though, also mean that there are very tiny swirls, riffles, and eddies interrupting the surface, and our contention is that the lighter tippet enables the fly to bounce and dance more naturally through those minute interruptions. It acts more like a natural insect adrift in the subtle currents.

But whatever the reason, sometimes the simple act of going to a smaller-diameter tippet will produce takes that you couldn't get otherwise. If you find that feeding fish won't take your fly and you're reasonably sure that you're matching the insects being eaten, try going to a smaller tippet, particularly in smooth, quiet water.

Leader length is also a serious consideration for the dry-fly fisher. Generally, anything less than 7½ feet is considered a short leader and anything over about 10 feet is considered a long leader. There are many good reasons for using the shortest leader that you can: (A) it's much easier to cast a shorter leader; (B) it is affected less by the wind; (C) it requires less power to get it to unroll properly; and (D) it is much easier to direct it to the exact spot where you wish the fly to land.

The advantages of a long leader include the following: the fly can light farther from the end of the line and from the disturbance caused by it, you have more built-in slack so that the fly can move more freely on the surface, and you can place the fly farther away without casting more line.

What length leader should you use? For most situations, a 7½-foot or 9-foot leader will work quite well, and you should stay within those bounds unless there is a particular reason to go to a longer leader.

Much like the rationale for using a smaller tippet, adding more tippet to get a longer leader sometimes produces results. Usually it's better to add a section of finer tippet material first, which automatically adds some length to the leader. You could, of course, change to a longer leader. It really doesn't matter which of the two produces a take as long as it does produce a take! Don and I both use an 8½- or 9-foot graphite rod, throwing a number 5, weight-forward fly line for our dry-fly fishing. We both generally use a 7½-foot, 4X or 5X leader to start with (most of our fishing requires #14 to #20 dries). Keep in mind that we do most of our fishing on Western streams where wind is the rule rather than the exception, and most of the water we fish is at least slightly broken. Under these conditions we rarely need light lines (they are actually a detriment in the wind), long leaders, and finer than normal tippets. Others who fish the same waters that we do use an entirely different set of equipment and catch just as many fish as we do. The important thing isn't what equipment you use, it is that the equipment is balanced and enables you to be successful with your style of fishing.

Fly Selection

This is the toughest part of fly-fishing. Casting may be difficult to learn, but once learned, it is accomplished without even thinking about it; reading water well is an art, achieved only through experience, but, again, it comes almost naturally after it's mastered. Fly selection, however, is always a conscious act.

The simplest, and often the most effective, method of deciding which fly to use is to observe carefully the insects on the water. Then select the fly that most closely resembles them. Silhouette (wing shape, body length, and so on), size, and color are the main considerations. (See Appendix A.)

Usually, silhouette is the first and most important criterion, but we have seen trout take any olive fly of the right size. The insects were mayflies, with upright wings, but a small stonefly imitation (over-the-back wing) worked every bit as well as a mayfly imitation. We have been fishing when the natural was a dark gray color, but any imitation of the right size and silhouette worked, regardless of color. And we've been there when the right color and silhouette was the "trigger" to the trout, and the size seemed irrelevant. If we had to list these factors in order of importance, we would probably say silhouette, size, and color, but not without a lot of qualifiers, because we've seen the rule broken too many times.

Sometimes things are really easy; the trout seem willing to take anything offered to them. Often we have fished in separate pools, taking fish easily, and were rather smug knowing that we had found which fly to use, only to meet later and find that we were using two totally different flies with equal success. Those days are rare, though. Usually the trout feed on one particular insect. When only one type of insect is hatching, it is called a simple hatch, according to Swisher and Richards in *Fly Fishing Strategy*. This situation is almost as easy as when the trout take anything you offer. Observation will quickly tell you which fly to use, and you will surely be successful.

When several different types, sizes, and colors of insects are on the water, it is very difficult to distinguish just which one, or ones, the trout is feeding on. Trout generally zero in on one particular insect when they are available in large numbers. If several different naturals are available in large numbers, they will still generally feed only on one particular type.

Swisher and Richards identify these situations as compound hatches and complex hatches. They define a compound hatch (or masking hatch) as one in which "the presence of a larger, more brightly colored insect effectively masks the presence of a much smaller, darker insect, which is almost imperceptible in the flow." They define a complex hatch as one in which a large number of many different types of insects are on the water at the same time. Either of these situations requires much more than a cursory look at what is on the water.

A couple of years ago, we hit the Middle Fork of the Platte regularly and did very well with several #14 mayfly imitations, which had dark brown bodies and tan wings. We arrived one day and tied on our flies at the truck before proceeding to the stream. After going fishless for a half hour or more, despite actively feeding trout everywhere, Don finally took the time to survey the water closely, and, although our mayfly was present in large numbers, so were some small, bright green stoneflies that we hadn't seen before. We switched flies and things immediately picked up. Later in the day, the trout started taking the brown mayflies, and again we wasted a half hour or so of prime fishing time before we caught on to the switch. Whether fishing a complex or compound hatch, you simply must be observant!

Every spring there is a tremendous hatch of caddisflies on Colorado's Arkansas River, and fly fishers come from all over the country to get in on the action. The hatch is so heavy at times that you can't even see the surface of the river, and cars on the highway along the river have to use their windshield wipers. Not much difficulty in knowing what fly to use, right? Well, almost all the time—but there's also a mayfly that hatches during this time, particularly if it gets overcast or starts raining. Now, the caddisfly is a #12 to a #16, and the mayfly (called a blue-winged olive or BWO) is a #18 or #20, yet if the BWO hatch comes off in the middle of the caddis hatch, the trout almost always switch over to feeding on it. Sure fools a lot of anglers, including us guides now and then. Fly shop owners get asked a hundred times a year, "Do you have any mayfly imitations?" They immediately know that there's a beginner in their midst. How? Simple. Any dry fly tied with an upright wing is a mayfly, and mayfly patterns probably make up 70% of their dry-fly selection. The ability to place aquatic insects into their large groups, called orders, is important to the fly fisher and really very simple.

MAYFLIES

The mayflies belong to the order of insects called Ephemeroptera (E-FEM-ER-OP-TUR-UH), meaning short-lived, winged. The adult mayfly is readily distinguishable by its upright wings (Illus. 5-1), like those of a butterfly. The mayflies are unique in that they go through two stages as adults. The newly hatched adult is called a subimago by entomologists (scientists who study insects) or a dun by fly fishers. The dun's body color is rather dull, and the wing is colored. After a period of time (from a few hours to a couple of days) the insect undergoes another molt and becomes an imago, or spinner, in fly-fishing

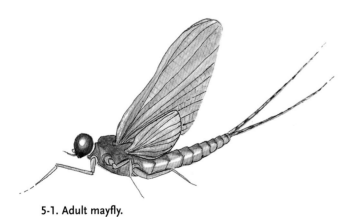

5-1. Adult mayfly.

parlance. The spinner has a much brighter coloration, and the wing is now clear. The subimago, or dun, stage is usually the most important to the fly fisher because the freshly hatched stage is most available to the trout. After swimming to the water's surface, the insect struggles in the surface film to crawl out of the nymphal husk. Once the adult insect is free of the nymphal case, it must ride the current for a short time waiting for the wings to unfold and stiffen sufficiently so that it can fly away. As you can see, it is very vulnerable to the trout during this drift down the river. The analogy has been used to the point of triteness, but the newly hatched adults look like diminutive sailboats, and, in fact, on a breezy day they get bounced around on the water by the wind striking their wings.

The mayfly duns move to the surrounding brush when able and remain there to undergo the molt into the imago, or spinner, stage. After molting, they return over the water where they mate in the air. After mating, the females fly with their abdomens dragging in the surface film to wash the eggs into the stream. Shortly after mating and laying the eggs, both the males and females die. At death, the wings relax into an outstretched position and many of the mayflies fall into the water. This is called a spinner fall, and at times the trout will feed very heavily on the expired insects.

CADDISFLIES

Caddisflies are placed in the order called Trichoptera (TRY-COP-TUR-UH), meaning hair-winged (the wings are covered by tiny hairs). Adult caddisflies are most recognizable by their wing shape (Illus. 5-2). They carry their wings extended over their backs in an inverted V, tent-shaped.

The caddisflies emerge through the surface film, much like the mayflies, although they can

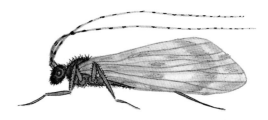

5-2. Adult caddisfly.

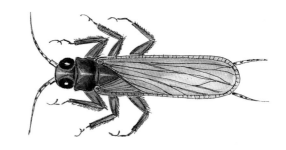

5-3. Adult stonefly.

become airborne much faster and aren't usually available to the trout as long as mayflies are. They quickly fly to surrounding brush for cover, where they will eventually mate. Unlike mayflies, which live only for a few days at the most, caddisflies may live as long as several weeks. The females return to the water to lay their eggs, with some species actually swimming to the stream bottom to place the eggs, while others drop their eggs in the surface film. Caddis adults also return to the stream to drink water and may become available to the trout during these times.

STONEFLIES

The stoneflies form the order named Plecoptera (PLAY-COP-TUR-UH), meaning pleated wing. Again, the wings of the adult are the most identifiable feature. Stoneflies carry their wings extended flat over their backs (Illus. 5-3).

Stoneflies don't emerge through the surface film like mayflies and caddisflies. The nymphs crawl out of the stream onto a rock, twig, or whatever, and the adult emerges there. Therefore, they aren't available to the trout as they emerge. The females do return to the water to deposit their eggs, either swimming under or washing the eggs off the abdomen in the surface film. They are, of course, available to the trout at these times, as well as when they return to take water. Stoneflies are clumsy fliers and often fall into the water while mating or as they crawl around on rocks and brush surrounding the stream.

MIDGES

The midges are in the order Diptera (DIP-TUR-UH), meaning two-winged. They are true flies and carry their wings in a flat V, the same shape as the common housefly (Illus. 5-4).

The majority of the midges are quite small, which has led fly fishers to refer to all very small aquatic insects as midges, even though the little rascals might really be caddisflies or mayflies. Sometimes midges are important to the fly fisher but not nearly as often as mayflies, caddisflies, or stoneflies.

If you are fascinated by the insects that the trout feed upon, you might want to consult one of the many excellent books on the subject. It is fun to collect insects, placing them in their appropri-

ate family and species, and to keep track of when they are likely to be found on your favorite streams, but it's not really necessary in order to be an effective fly fisher. If you know the difference between the orders then you can establish an appropriate silhouette for your imitation, and then you only have to match the color and size to "match the hatch." After convincing you that you must see what insects are hatching in order to duplicate them as closely as you can, I'll now get to the exceptions (yes, there are always exceptions).

What do you do when there just isn't a hatch occurring? In this case the trout are probably not feeding selectively on a particular insect, but that doesn't necessarily mean that they aren't feeding. Ants, grasshoppers, bees, crickets, deerflies, horseflies, moths, and other terrestrial insects are likely to be eaten when available. They aren't going to be on the water in great numbers on most days, so kick around in the undergrowth, shake a few bushes, and look around in the vegetation to see what is most likely to end up accidentally in the water.

A friend and I spent most of one afternoon trying to take a particularly large trout on the Eagle River. The railway running along the edge of the pool is 10 feet or so above the water, and from that vantage point you can see every fish.

We had been taking turns; one of us "coached" from up on the railway bed while the other followed directions and cast to the trout. After trying just about every imitation that we had without success, we gave up and went up to the Jeep. We opened a couple of cold sodas and sat down on the edge of the railway, salving our wounds. After swatting at and cursing the "damn grasshoppers" that kept banging into us, I finally saw the light—grasshoppers! (I've never been

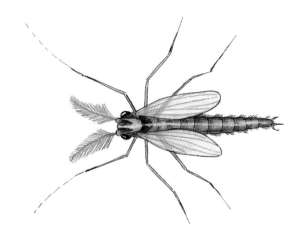

5-4. Adult midge.

accused of catching on quickly.) Tying on my best 'hopper pattern, I scrambled down the bank. By the time I started false-casting, Mike had located the trout.

"Another three feet, now two, just right," he said. The fly landed with a nice "smack" on the water, and as it started drifting, Mike felt the need to keep me informed.

"He sees it, he's turning, he's coming up, he's following it," and at the same second that I saw the trout headed for the fly, he screamed, "He's got it!" After all that build-up, I was so tense that when I saw the fish and he screamed, I set the hook. The fly skittered across the water for 3 or 4 feet and then became airborne, with the trout practically snapping at it all the way.

It doesn't really matter whether we took the trout or not (it mattered then, though). We had finally figured out the obvious: when grasshoppers are around, try using a grasshopper imitation.

In other situations, you may choose not to use your best imitation of the naturals on the water. In order to take fish consistently on dry flies, you must be able to see the fly. You should be able to see that it is drifting in the right feeding lane and that it isn't dragging across the current. And you need to know exactly where it is so that you can tell if the rise is to your fly or to a natural.

When the water takes on a dead slate color under an overcast sky, that small, dark-colored imitation may be impossible to see. Just at dusk, when the sun is low in the sky, the water often just sparkles, with the sunlight dancing off the riffles. It's beautiful, but it sure makes it hard to follow that light-colored, white-winged fly. In the first case I might choose a fly that has the silhouette, size, and body color of the natural, but with a white wing to increase its visibility. A dark,

heavily dressed fly is probably easier to recognize in the sparkling water. True, your imitation may not be a perfect match for the natural insect now, but since you can see the fly, you will be able to make a much better presentation. We can only hope that one offsets the other.

We all often have trouble seeing small flies, particularly if there is a lot of glare. The technique for those situations isn't new, but it sure works. When we tie on our tippet material, we intentionally leave 6 or 8 inches sticking out of the blood knot. Then we tie a large, brightly colored fly on that end. A second fly tied in above the end of the tippet like this is called a dropper, and the whole two-fly setup is called a cast of flies. That way, we have a fly that we can see within a foot or two of the imitative pattern that we are using. We can follow the fly's drift and accurately estimate if a rise is to our fly. As a bonus, we occasionally take a fish on the dropper. Often we go to a shorter leader so that the fly is closer to the end of the fly line, and we use the line tip to sort of point to the fly.

Another trick is to make a really short cast so that the fly is close enough you can see it and observe how it looks on the water. Is it darker than the water, lighter? Now that you've seen it up close, you know what to look for when you make your normal cast.

Reading the Water

There are as many different kinds of dry-fly water as there are stream sections in the country, and often we become intimidated because we are fishing somewhere other than our home haunts. The real key to being able to read water well and take fish consistently is the ability to interpret the "new" water in terms of what you are used to

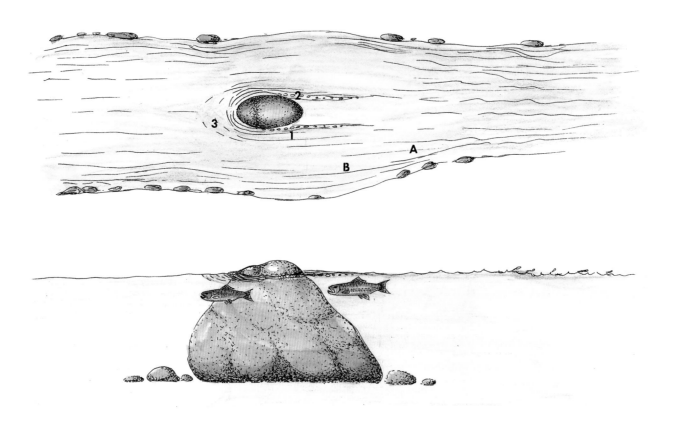

5-5. Overhead (top) and profile views of two lies.

seeing. There aren't really that many unique sections of water; it's just that the runs, pockets, and pools are arranged differently from those we are familiar with. Let's take a look at some typical sections of stream and analyze how we would approach them with rod in hand. We show two views of two common lies (Illus. 5-5): the overhead view and a profile or side view. Since it is preferable to move upstream when fishing dries, starting from the lower sections of the pool, the first approach should be from casting position A. The first really good lie in this stretch is directly behind the rock.

Because there is a fast section of water coming around the side of the rock nearest me, I would need to use a curve cast, S-cast, or some means of adding some slack to my line to get a good drift out of the fly before the fast water

catches my line and causes the fly to drag. My first cast would be from point A to point 1. I want to make my first drift along the edge of the faster water that is closer to me. My next drift would be made so that the fly is about halfway between the edge of the fast water and the rock; and the final drift through that spot would be with the fly right up against the rock. The second area that I would cover would be the edge of the run-out on the far side of the rock. After drifting the fly several times through the run on my side of the rock, I would cast from point A to point 2. I want to get my fly to drift along the edge between the fast and slow water on the far edge of the run-out.

Having drifted my fly several times as outlined above, I would quietly move up to casting position B in order to cover the lies on the front edge of the rock. The first cast should be on the

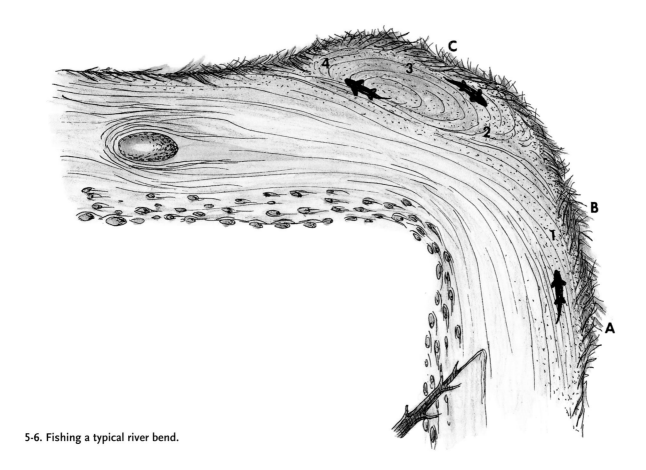

5-6. Fishing a typical river bend.

near edge of the fast water coming around my side of the rock; the second drift should be a little farther over into the fast water; and the third float should be along the inside edge of the fast water.

Be sure to take time to cover a section of water by starting close in and then extending your cast only a foot or two each time so that you cover all of the water. This is particularly important in a situation like the one above. The best lie, and the one that most likely holds a good fish, is behind the rock. The temptation is to make the first cast into that area. To do that, however, would mean that we might cast across three or four trout between our position and the fish behind the rock. Not only are those three or four trout that we won't have the opportunity to catch, but they might very well spook the fish behind the rock as they scatter away from the disturbance caused by the line.

In Illus. 5-6 is a rather typical bend in a river. Note that the water in the bend itself is actually flowing in the opposite direction from the stream's flow. This means that you have to pay attention to where your line is, where you expect the trout to be, and how to avoid drag. I would start fishing this bend from position A, using a normal, upstream presentation to point 1. I would make the first drift through the section with my fly close in against the edge of the bank. I would want my fly a couple of feet out from the edge on the next drift through, and the fly on the edge away from me during the third drift. Again, always work the fly from near to far so you don't spook any trout between where you stand and where you cast.

Next, I would move up to position B and start casting into the area marked 2. My first casts would be into a position where the fly would come back towards me on either edge of the fast water. Then I would extend my casts so that the fly would drift away from me, along the edge of the bank in the eddy. I'd have to use an S-cast or stop cast in order for the fly to drift away from me without drag.

After working as much of the eddy as possible from there, I would move up to position C and cast to the area around positions 3 and 4. Eddies like these are very productive because they provide many different lies and good protection for the trout. They are rather difficult to fish sometimes, though, because the water flows in several directions, and it can be difficult getting drag-free

float. Take your time in working areas like this—they always hold fish!

One thing to watch for is a foam line. It's pretty simple . . . if the foam is forming along a particular line, any food that's on the water will get moved into the same line by the current. Foam lines are always worth a drift or two.

Another productive area is shown in Illus. 5-7. If some of the rocks are large enough to provide protection for the trout, there might even be some primary lies in water of this type. Even if the rocks are smaller and don't provide the protection needed for a primary or resting lie, this type of water is often good for feeding lies. Because the stream narrows and accelerates

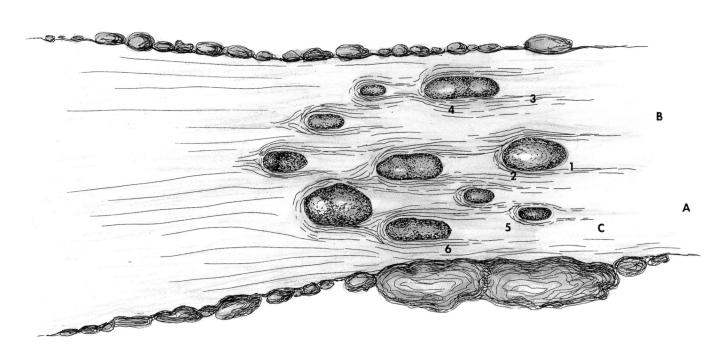

5-7. Fishing pocket water.

through the section, food becomes concentrated. Additionally, the many rocks in the area break up the water's flow and provide several pockets where the trout can lie in wait for his food without expending too much energy. This water type is called pocket water.

I would approach this stretch by weaving back and forth across the stream, working the slicks at the backs and sides of the rocks, until I had covered all areas that could be reached easily. Then, working upstream, I would drift the fly into the edges where the water breaks around the front of each rock. I would cast from A into areas 1 and 2, move to B and cast to 3 and 4, and so on. In some areas, I could probably float the fly more effectively by letting it drift downstream into the pockets. Because the water is flowing rapidly through this relatively shallow area, we needn't be too quiet in our approach. The water breaking over and around the rocks creates a lot of noise, and the trout isn't nearly as apt to sense our presence. By the same token, the broken surface of the water disrupts the trout's view of the surface, so that the fly doesn't have to imitate the insects on the water as closely. Gee, it sounds as if we have everything going for us in this pocket-water fishing, doesn't it? Not really!

What makes this fishing tough is that the pockets and runs where we want to float the fly are very small. It takes good, accurate casting in order to get the needed drifts through those short, fast runs around the rocks. And getting a drag-free float in this water where we have a plethora of water speeds is really tough! This is exciting fishing, though. It takes rapid-fire casting to keep the fly on the water, and since the drifts are short and fast, the trout really tear into the flies. Once the fish is on the line, he has the advantage of the fast water to use against our efforts to land him, not to mention a vast choice of rocks to tangle us in. Fun stuff! There are, of course, an unlimited number of water types and situations that we could show you, but these few should illustrate the main points of how to approach a stream when fishing dry flies.

1. The casting position is critical. You must get the fly into the right area without drag.

2. You must be able to recognize those areas where the trout are likely to be when feeding; generally they will be found on the edges—the edges between fast and slow water, edges of obstructions, or the edges of the stream, because that is where the food will accumulate.

3. Cast as short a line as possible to increase accuracy and to better control the line on the water's surface. Fishing dry flies is probably the most exciting way to take trout, but it isn't the most effective on a day-in, day-out basis. For every adult insect that the trout takes from the surface of the water, he probably takes 10 or 12 insects in the nymphal or larval stage beneath the surface.

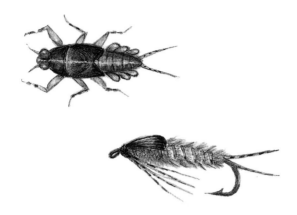

NYMPHING IT

I f you really want to be able to take trout under almost any conditions, nymphing is the way to do it. The underwater stages of the aquatic insects are available to the trout at virtually all times and, therefore, form the bulk of their diet. Although nymphing isn't considered by most fly fishers as much fun as fishing dry flies, it is a much more consistent method of taking fish.

Dry-fly fishing is most productive when a hatch is in progress. Limiting yourself to fishing only during those periods will certainly restrict how much time you spend catching fish. One benefit of nymph fishing is that it effectively extends the fishing season. Here in Colorado, our fishing season is open year round, and by fishing nymphs during the colder months, when very few hatches occur, we can take advantage of the entire year.

Remember the paradox of dry-fly fishing? Although it is the easiest method, it is also the most difficult. Well, nymphing fits into the same mold. It's very simple because you don't need to be able to cast well; leader length and tippet size, although important, aren't nearly as critical as when fishing dry flies; and presentation just isn't as difficult. On the other hand, trying to make a correct fly presentation down near the bottom of the stream where you can't see what is going on isn't all that easy. It's a bit more difficult to decide which fly to use when fishing nymphs because there are many food forms available, like a complex hatch all the time. But what really makes nymph fishing hard is the difficulty in detecting when the trout takes the fly.

Equipment for Nymphing

RODS

Most serious nymph fishermen seem to prefer a long fly rod. The most effective method is the tight-line technique, in which there is almost no line on the water: the line drapes from the end of the rod to the water's surface, and a long rod provides a longer reach. An 8-foot rod is about the shortest most nymph fishermen consider, and 9- or 9½-foot rods are common.

A rather soft, very sensitive rod action is probably the best for nymphing so that any strike by the trout is transmitted to the fisherman both by seeing the tip of the rod move and by feeling the take.

LINE, LEADER, TIPPET

Since very little casting is involved in most nymphing, line weight isn't critical, and many nymph fishermen like light lines: 4-, 5-, and 6-weight.

Long leaders are rarely needed when fishing nymphs; even a 7½-foot leader may be longer than you want. Most of the time when fishing nymphs you will need to add some weight to the leader (using split shot, lead substitute wire, or some other means), and you aren't going to get that leader to unroll with the weight on it. Tippet size, then, isn't critical in that regard, and the nymph fisherman often uses a smaller tippet than the Rule of Four dictates. A fine tippet probably doesn't keep the trout from seeing that the fly is attached to something, but you do want the fly to move as freely as possible. Using a small tippet gives the fly much more freedom of movement as it drifts through the water.

Flies

Selecting which fly to use can be a problem when conditions indicate that a nymph is called for, because the naturals aren't out flying around where you can observe them. If hatches have been coming off during the day, you can assume that the nymphal stage of those particular insects is active in the stream and you should try a suitable imitation. If there just isn't any insect activity to give you a clue, you need to get down in the stream and see what is happening or, at least, see what food forms are most prevalent. Pick up some rocks and observe the insects that you find there. You'll probably see several different kinds and sizes on each rock, but by looking at several, you will get some idea which ones are available in the greatest numbers. Also be on the lookout for the unusual.

Don called one early spring day to tell me that the fishing was pretty hot down on the Arkansas River and that the trout were really turned on to stonefly nymphs. The predominant stonefly in the stretches where we fish is the golden stonefly (*Acroneuria californica*), so I tied up a few using a bright yellow yarn and ribbed it with a clear, light brown Swannundaze. They were very pretty but seemed awfully bright, even to represent the amber-colored stonefly. Don scoffed a bit when I showed him what I had brought along. He had a similar tie, but its color was much more subdued. My son, Lance, and I started taking trout immediately, and, although Don was picking up a fish now and then, the Golden Stonefly pattern was getting takes at least two to one over Don's pattern.

If you hear Don tell the story, he nearly drowned getting down on his knees in the middle of the Arkansas to beg for a fly. To set the record

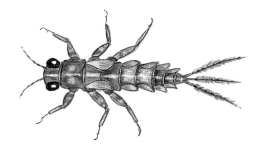

6-1. Mayfly nymph.

straight, I didn't make him get down on his knees and only insisted that he grovel for a couple of minutes before I gave him one.

We caught a lot of trout that day. After taking enough to be satisfied for a while, we began plucking rocks from the stream bed to see if there was any explanation for the success of these very brightly colored flies. Sure enough, we found a scattering of stonefly nymphs that were almost entirely a bright buttercup yellow. We later called our friend Gary LaFontaine, who cleared up the question for us. It seems that as the nymph grows, it keeps outgrowing its exoskeleton; therefore it sheds it (molts). The bright yellow nymphs we were finding were those who were in the instar, or stage before their new exoskeletons had formed. Eric Leiser and Bob Boyle reported a similar experience with white stonefly nymphs (*Rod & Reel* magazine, March 1982). Apparently the unusual color of these nymphs in their helpless state is a strong trigger to the trout. Needless to say, the bright yellow stonefly nymph has become one of our standard nymph patterns on the Arkansas.

The flies that you need are, of course, imitative of the underwater stages of the same four orders of insects that we talked about when discussing dry flies: mayflies, caddisflies, stoneflies, and midges.

MAYFLIES (EPHEMEROPTERA)

The mayflies go through an incomplete metamorphosis (egg, nymph, and adult stages), so the underwater stage is a true nymph. The nymphs vary in color considerably, but most are shades of grey, olive, or brown and appear rather drab. Their size may range from ¾ inch long to ⅜ inch long. The silhouette of a good mayfly nymph imitation should include two or three tails, a segmented abdomen, legs, and a wing case (Illus. 6-1).

CADDISFLIES (TRICHOPTERA)

The caddisflies undergo a complete metamorphosis consisting of egg, larval, pupal, and adult stages. Notice that there isn't a nymphal stage; the fly fisher is really imitating the larva or pupa of the insect (Illus. 6-2) even though we call the imitation a nymph and consider the fishing method nymphing.

The majority of the caddis larvae develop inside a case, a sort of cocoon, made of small stones, leaves, or other vegetation, which the insect constructs around itself and attaches to a rock or twig. Others (called free-living) build and tend nests for feeding or attach themselves to underwater rocks or twigs with a strand of "silk." The transformation of the insect from the larval to the pupal stage occurs inside a case, sealed except for a tiny hole for water to trickle through. After pupation, the adult caddis (Illus. 6-3) gnaws its way out of the case and rises to the surface in a membranous sac.

Trout readily take caddis larvae and pupae by rooting the cases from their attachment, in the instance of the cased species, or by waiting for the free-living types to wash from their moorings. The feeding spree occurs, though, when the adults start rising to the surface. Upon maturity,

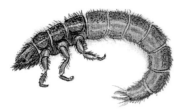

6-2. Caddisfly larva.

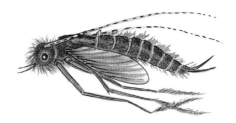

6-3. Caddisfly emerger.

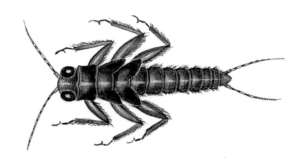

6-4. Stonefly nymph.

the adult caddis generates gas inside the membranous sac and rides the gas-filled "bubble" to the surface. It is totally exposed to the trout during the journey and thus is most vulnerable to predation.

The free-living caddis vary in shades of olive, cream, and tan to dark brown and gray. The case color of the case-building species varies depending on the material used for the construction of the case. The common caddis larva and pupa range in size from approximately ¹⁄₁₆ inch long to ¾ inch long. The emerging caddis carry the color of the adult, although from the trout's viewpoint through the membranous sac the color appears duller. What is significant, however, about the emerging caddis is not its color. The sac surrounding the insect contains a bubble of gas, and that rising bubble reflects light, appearing as a spot of light rising to the surface. The most realistic imitation of the emerging adult is achieved by using the Sparkle Pupa patterns developed by Gary LaFontaine. These patterns are tied with a trilobal yarn, which actually captures a bubble of air within it to achieve the same "spot of light" appearance as the natural insect. Beadhead nymphal patterns are also very effective, as the weight of the bead gets the nymph quickly to a fishing depth in the stream, and light reflecting from the bead may represent the air bubble to the trout.

STONEFLIES (PLECOPTERA)

The stoneflies go through an incomplete metamorphosis, so there is a true nymphal stage. The stonefly nymphs (Illus. 6-4) look very similar to the mayfly nymphs. The major differences are that the stonefly is much more robust, usually larger, and has two wing cases instead of the one found on the mayfly nymph.

Stoneflies breathe through external appendages on their bodies and thus are usually found in the faster sections of water on the stream, where the oxygen content is high. Unlike the mayflies, they don't hatch by swimming to the surface and emerging from their nymphal cases; they crawl out of the stream and emerge in the atmosphere. They are rather active in the stream, however, and are often available to the trout.

The stone fly nymphs vary in size from ¼ inch to 2 inches long. Their coloration runs the gamut from dusky amber, to reddish brown, to olive through olive brown, to nearly black.

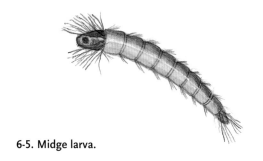

6-5. Midge larva.

MIDGES (DIPTERA)

Midges develop through a complete metamorphosis: egg, larva, pupa, and adult. The larval and pupal stages are the ones that the nymph fly fisher is concerned with. This order includes mosquitoes, no-see-ums, tsetse flies, buffalo gnats, and blackflies among its notorious members. It also includes innocuous species, such as gnats and crane flies. As the name implies, most members of this order are small; many pupae are less than 1/32 inch long, which would require hooks smaller than #28 to imitate. The larger species are the ones that the fly fisher is primarily concerned with: some of the larger true midges, the mosquitoes, and the crane flies.

The larvae of the midges are wormlike in appearance and are found in almost every color but generally aren't available to the trout (Illus. 6-5). The pupation may occur free-floating in the water, in a cocoonlike case in or out of the water, in a gelatinous case, or in moist soil along the stream bank. The free-floating species, such as the mosquitoes, are of considerable importance to the fly fisher when the pupae hang in the water, powerless to escape. Fishing midge pupae is nearly identical to fishing dry flies; the imitation must be presented with no drag, because the insects in the pupal state are incapable of much movement. Their coloration may be gray, cream, olive, orangish, or tan, probably depending to some extent on what they have been eating.

Now, all you need to do is to capture some specimens of the prevalent insects in your stream, match one with a reasonable imitation, and start catching trout, right? But what if you are going to a stream you haven't fished before and haven't the foggiest idea of what insects are present? There are a couple of possible solutions to that problem. Call ahead to a fly shop in the area and inquire about the insect activity and which patterns you should bring with you. Or better yet, plan on stopping by the shop and buying a few of the local patterns and getting the free information about what's going on where. Barring that, there are several very good books on the market that contain "emergence tables." These charts are for different areas of the country, and they outline the normal time periods for the particular hatches of aquatic insects. They aren't absolutely accurate because local weather and water conditions may vary, but they will serve as a guide to insects that might be active during your visit.

Nymphing Techniques

Successful nymph-fishing methods vary from the tight-line technique, where virtually no line is on the water, to the floating-nymph technique, which is nearly identical to dry-fly fishing. Which method you should use is dependent on many factors, including water conditions, type of fly, and most important, the insect activity. The techniques are also regional. Around our part of the country the tight-line technique is, far and away, the most used. This regionality is rather unfortunate because it should be obvious that the techniques that work in Colorado are sure to be successful at times in Pennsylvania, and the California methods will undoubtedly catch trout in Montana. Those barriers are being eroded as fly fishers across the nation have more and more avenues for communication through the many fly-fishing magazines and books on the market, as well as the Internet. Let's take a look at the different methods and see which are best suited for certain conditions.

TIGHT-LINE TECHNIQUE

Also called the outrigger method, this is the most common technique used here in Colorado and lends itself to fast, deep runs where the nymph must be presented dead-drift, near the bottom. It requires a floating fly line, a rather short leader, a fine tippet, and some weight on the leader. The weight, in the form of lead substitute wire, strips, or split shot, is attached to the leader approximately 18 inches above the fly. This weighting of the leader is necessary in order to get the fly down to the bottom reaches of the stream in fast water. We probably couldn't get enough weight on the fly to be effective. Besides, most of us feel that a heavily weighted fly loses some of its natural movement.

Now, you don't cast this rig! That weighted leader simply won't form a good casting loop, and either the weight or the fly might remove your earlobe. It is strictly a short-line technique, and what line you do need is cast in a huge overhand wide loop. Because the fish have difficulty detecting anglers in fast, heavy water, you don't need to be overly concerned about standing too close to where the fish are. In fact, it isn't uncommon to take fish within a couple of feet of where you have been standing for a while.

To fish the tight-line method, wade out to within a rod length or so of the suspected feeding or holding lie. Use a very wide overhand loop to lob the fly nearly straight upstream. Immediately raise the rod tip so that the line is kept taut between the tip of the rod and the weight on the leader. Usually, the depth is adjusted with the rod tip so that you can feel the weight tap the bottom as it drifts. As the fly drifts towards you, lift the rod tip to keep the line tight, and then start lowering the tip so that the drift of the fly is not impeded as it moves on below you. As with any nymphing technique, the difficult part is detecting a strike. Many nymph fishermen use a strike indicator to assist in seeing the take. A small cork painted with fluorescent paint, a short section of floating fly line, or a manufactured, bright-colored strip of foam rubber can be attached to the leader at a point where it will be just in the surface film when the fly reaches the proper depth. The indicator must be watched intently during the entire drift and the rod tip lifted to set the hook at the slightest movement of the indicator. It isn't going to be pulled under suddenly like a bait-fishing bobber! Usually the only indication of a take will be a slight pause in the indicator's movement downstream, or a very subtle side movement of an inch or so, or, perhaps, a slight speed-up of the indicator in relation to the water's speed.

If you closely watch a skilled practitioner of the tight-line method, you will notice that he lifts the rod tip and sets the hook repeatedly during the drift. This is because it is impossible to detect the difference between the fly bumping something underwater or a trout bumping his fly. The only way to be certain that it was or wasn't a fish is to set the hook each and every time the indicator moves.

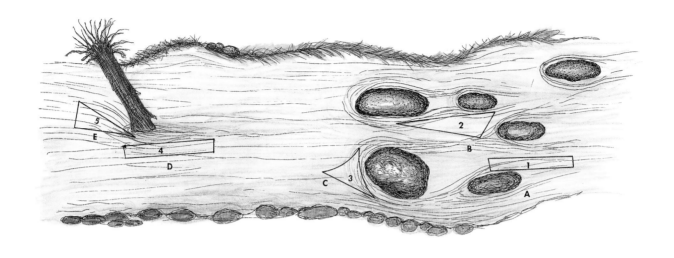

6-6. Typical tight-line nymphing water.

Here are a couple of typical situations in which you might use the tight-line technique.

As you can see from Illus. 6-6, the primary zones for drifting the nymph are areas of maximum water flow, particularly if the flow passes close to a quiet section of water. In this kind of stream, you would stand at A and cast to 1, at B and cast to 2, and so on. The fast, concentrated water flow ensures that the available food will all pass through that narrow area. And if the trout can hold on the edge of the fast water and avoid having to swim in it all the time, he will be in there feeding.

FLOATING NYMPH METHOD

When the trout feed on emerging nymphs just under the surface, this is the tactic that will do them in. The method is almost identical to fishing the dry fly, both because of the way the imitation is presented and because you are fishing to a visible fish. In this case, the trout isn't taking the insects from the surface, so there isn't a true riseform. What we are seeing is the bulge created by the trout's back as he swirls to take the nymph, just under the surface.

The casting and line handling are the same as when fishing dries, and the technique is only slightly more difficult. The only increase in difficulty arises when you can't see your fly and must keep track of where the leader is so you can judge if the bulge of the trout is to your nymph. A floating line, a normal length leader (7 ½ to 9 feet) that has been treated with floatant to within 6 or 8 inches of the fly, a fine tippet, and a pupal imitation that creates some movement in the water are the key ingredients to the system. Putting a larger dry fly on the tippet and then tying a couple of feet of tippet material from the bend of that hook to your nymph will give you a great indicator for detecting a strike. And, maybe, you'll even get a take on the dry fly!

Just as in fishing dries, you must remember to cast so that the fly lands above the trout and has time to sink to the correct depth by the time it reaches his feeding position.

LEISENRING LIFT

This technique can be employed with some success in conjunction with any of the other nymphing methods. The whole idea is to drift the fly to a spot directly in front of the trout and then suddenly raise it towards the surface right in front of his nose (Illus. 6-7).

Because the technique is dependent on causing the fly to suddenly jump towards the surface at the correct time, it requires that you either drift the nymph to a visible fish or into a known lie. As you might imagine, the technique is deadly but relatively difficult to pull off successfully. The toughest part is to cast the fly where it will drift into the correct position and arrive at the correct depth at the same time.

SUNKEN-LINE TECHNIQUE

This is, undoubtedly, the most difficult method of fishing the nymph and is appropriate only for a certain water type: relatively slow, deep water with few obstructions. The sunken-line technique requires a full sinking line or a sinking-tip line and a rather short leader with a fine tippet. The difficulty is in detecting the strike. Because the line, leader, and fly are all below the surface, it is difficult to tell when the trout takes the fly. In fact, the most common indication is a slight pause in the movement of the line, or, if

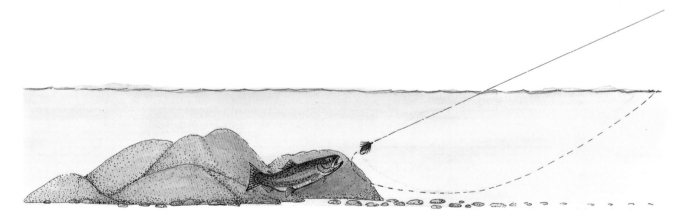

6-7. The Leisenring lift.

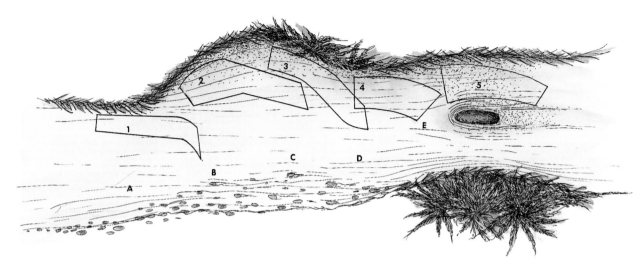

6-8. Casting progression on a stream.

you're lucky, a flash given off by the trout as he turns on the fly. Cast the fly upstream so that the line sinks by the time the fly passes the suspected holding or feeding lie (Illus. 6-8). As with any of the methods, the first cast should cover the water closest to you; each subsequent cast should cover the next section of water. In a stream like the one in Illus. 6-8, you would cast from A to 1, from A to 2, and so on. Moving downstream, you would cast from B to points 1 through 5. You would do the same for all points through E. Since the intent is to get the fly down near the bottom of the stream, you must keep the leader short; otherwise it will tail up too far from the bottom.

DRY AND DROPPER TECHNIQUE

Here's a method that combines dry-fly and nymph fishing and is the most consistent producer we have found. Choose a dry fly that represents a common insect on the stream and tie it on your leader just as if dry-fly fishing. Now tie 30 to 36 inches of 5X tippet (called a dropper, remember?) right on the bend of that hook. Add a beadhead nymph on the end of the dropper and start just as if fishing the dry fly only. Now, of course you might take a trout on either fly, but that dry fly will act as a great strike indicator if you get a take on the nymph. You've essentially doubled your chances of catching a fish!

Many other techniques might be used to take trout on a nymph, and many of those are combinations of the ones we have discussed. The important thing to remember, though, is that your fly must represent a natural food form to the trout, and you must use a method of presentation that will appear natural in the type of water you are fishing. Nymph fishing is, in many ways, the most difficult form of fly-fishing. But it is well worth mastering because it is the most effective way to catch trout.

LITTLE FISHES

Streamer fishing is truly an endeavor of little fishes, not the ones that we are catching, but the ones we are imitating. A streamer fly is an imitation of a minnow or small fish in the stream. Because we are representing a rather large creature, our streamers are generally the largest flies that we use. And, because the little fishes are lively, we usually impart some movement to our imitations. In short, streamer fishing is considerably different from dry-fly or nymph fishing. To be a successful streamer fisherman, you must be able to envision (A) how a small fish moves in the stream; (B) what you must do with your rod and line to imitate that movement; and (C) where you should put the fly in order to entice a strike.

Fishing streamers requires most of the techniques and abilities of both the dry-fly fisherman and the nymph fisherman. Like the nymph fisherman, you must be able to control the fly in three dimensions (length, width, depth) and be able to read the water in order to present the fly in a natural manner. But there is one thing that makes streamer fishing easier than nymphing: you won't have any difficulty detecting the strike. The trout will attack your fly as though it were a fast-moving, darting minnow, and when he hits the streamer, you'll know it!

There are a couple of reasons that trout take a streamer. The obvious is that they are taking it as food; another is that they are protecting their territory, particularly during the spawning season.

This latter reason is one which often gives the angler some real thrills. If you can find a section of river above a reservoir or lake that holds large trout, you will get some amazing action during the spawning season. What happens is the large fish that are resident in the lake move up into the stream to spawn (browns and brookies in the fall; rainbows and cutthroats in the spring), and, although they don't feed much during the spawn, they do become very protective of the nests, or redds, as they are called. A large streamer resembling an invading fish, right down on the bottom among the redds, will bring some slashing strikes as the spawners try to protect the eggs. This type of fishing is chancy because it must coincide with the arrival of the large spawners from the lake. But if you are in the right place at the right time, you will be thrilled again and again, by catching trout up to three or four times the size of the residents in the river.

Even when fishing for resident fish, the streamer fisherman will generally take larger trout than someone who is nymphing or fishing dry flies. The larger the trout become, the more they become predatory on smaller fish in the stream. Minnows simply provide more energy than insects, and the trout's instinct for survival predicates that it can't expend more energy obtaining food than it derives from it. Big trout eat insect forms when available in large enough quantities to consume with little effort. It takes a lot of mayfly nymphs to equal the food energy of one minnow. As a result, minnows make up a greater portion of a large trout's diet.

Equipment for Streamer Fishing

Certainly, any outfit suitable for fishing dries or nymphs can suffice for the streamer fisherman. But if you get serious about pursuing trout with streamers, you can gear your equipment towards the larger (and often weighted) flies that you will be casting, and the larger fish that you are likely to be pitted against.

RODS

An 8- to 9-foot rod will give you a bit more reach, which will come in handy when trying to impart some realistic action to the streamer. Since the flies are larger and heavier, casting will be somewhat easier if you use a heavier line weight than usual for fishing dry flies. A 6-weight rod would be in the light range for a streamer rod, and an 8-weight wouldn't be unreasonable. A large, heavy streamer just doesn't lend itself to a delicate presentation. Besides, when fishing streamers we usually cast to a position well away from the holding or feeding lie of the trout and let the current carry our offering into position as it sinks to the proper depth.

LINE, LEADER, TIPPET

When fishing streamers, you don't want a long leader with a fine tippet. On the contrary, a long leader simply lets the fly tail up from the bottom in the current instead of keeping the streamer down near the bottom where it usually belongs. It's not unusual to use only a 3- or 4-foot leader to offset that problem; it also makes controlling the swimming action of the imitation easier.

Fly Selection

In some ways, selecting the right fly is more difficult when fishing streamers than when fishing dries and nymphs, because minnow type (size and color) is harder to determine than insect activity. Probably the most important aspect of imitation when using streamers is movement. Color and size are sometimes important, but even if the color and size are right, the fly won't entice very many fish if it doesn't have the movement and flash of a natural minnow.

This was certainly the case a few summers ago when I was after salmon in Alaska. I was fishing on the Newhalen River just a couple of miles from the Iliamna Lake Lodge, where I was staying. The sockeyes were just starting their run into the river and were bright and fresh from the sea. I was able to take them on virtually any color and size of fly, as long as it was tied using a very soft wing material. Tinsel, although not as definite a preference, provided flash, which also seemed important. We prefer not to use weighted streamers because a weighted fly of any sort loses some of its natural bounce and liveliness, and in a streamer that lifelike movement is critical. We usually add some weight to the leader if we don't need to get too deep; or we use a sinking-tip line if necessary to get down deep enough. If fishing really big, heavy water, we occasionally even go to a full-sinking line.

Some streamer types are almost universal throughout the country: the Muddler Minnow; the Little Brown Trout and Little Rainbow Trout patterns; the Light and Dark Spruce Flies; the Spuddler; and the Matuka (Illus. 7-1 through 7-5). You should carry all of these in sizes from #2 to #10, and you should carry Muddlers and Matukas in several colors as well. If we had to choose just two streamers to carry, they would be the Muddlers and the Matukas. The original Muddler was all brown, but it is now often tied as a Marabou Muddler, using marabou of several different colors. This pattern is so versatile that it imitates almost any small fish and has even saved the day for me a time or two as a grasshopper imitation. The Matuka-style streamer has been around for many, many years but had been largely forgotten until Swisher and Richards (*Fly Fishing Strategy*)

7-1. Little Brown Trout.

7-2. Little Rainbow Trout.

7-3. Spuddler.

7-4. Black/yellow Matuka.

7-5. Spruce Fly.

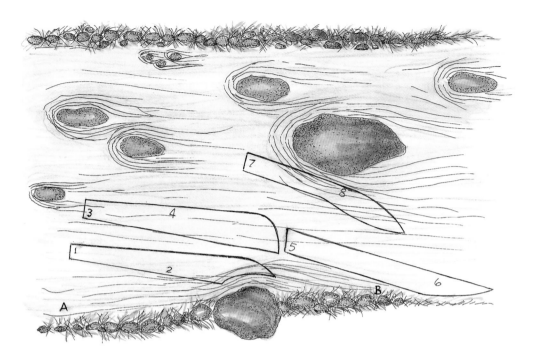

7-6. Typical streamer water.

brought it to everyone's attention again. The real advantage to the Matuka-style streamer is that you get a good wing silhouette (the wing on a streamer actually forms the body of the fly), it gives good movement, and you don't end up with the hackle wing caught under the bend of the hook. The most effective color combinations we have found are cream with a black wing, olive with a grizzly wing, and black with an olive wing. (See Streamers, in Appendix A.)

Casting

Let's head for the stream now and see if we can drum up some of those lunkers that are looking for a dinner of little fishes. The first drawing (Illus. 7-6) shows a typical pocket-water stretch of a river. In this case, the water in most spots isn't deep enough to warrant casting so that the fly has time to really get deep. The primary lies and the

holding lies tell us where we want to put our offering.

This section of stream is probably best worked by casting slightly up and across stream. From casting position A, I would make my first cast to position 1 so that the fly will be down near the bottom of the stream by the time it gets to point 2. Many, if not most, of the strikes will come just as the fly makes its swing across current at the end of the drift. Next, I would cast to position 3 so the fly swings into position 4 at the completion of the drift. By slightly lengthening each cast, I could work this whole section of the stream without casting over any water not already fished.

By moving to position B, I could cast to point 5 to drift into position 6, cast to 7 to drift into 8, and so on. By methodically working my way down the stream in this manner, I can present my streamer in each of the primary and holding lies.

7-7. Fishing streamers in pocket water, overhead and side view.

Often, the coup de grace is achieved by giving the streamer a Leisenring lift just as it drifts into the lie. This sudden darting movement of the fly will often entice a smashing strike, just as it does when fishing nymphs.

The second stream situation (Illus. 7-7) is a large, rather deep, fast-moving section of river. This might well be a section above a reservoir, like the one I mentioned earlier. One of the problems in this kind of water is getting the fly down deep enough, and, if we are looking at this as a possible spawning situation, it does need to be right down in the rocks on the bottom of the stream.

I could, of course, overcome some of the difficulty by going to a sinking-tip or full sinking line. Even with that, I would need to cast well upstream from where I wish the fly to be at full depth, so that it will have time to sink as it drifts down to where I perceive the fish to be. There's a very important, yet simple, principle at work here:

the deeper the fly needs to be, the farther upstream you must make your cast.

In Illus. 7-7 are two views of the same stream. The stream bed is made up of rocks, baseball-size and smaller, with an occasional large boulder—an ideal spawning area.

Here, I would start by casting from position A to point 1. Notice how far upstream I place the fly. That's so it will have time to sink clear to the bottom before reaching a point directly across from me. Although I am casting to a point well upstream, I'm actually fishing the water from a point directly across stream and down. I would make that drift two or three times and then aim my cast to position 2. After casting to point 2 two or three times, I'd cast to point 3, and so on. Again, by casting fairly close to where I'm standing and then making each presentation a little farther out, I'm casting across water that I have already fished.

Occasionally, a fish will take a streamer as it is "dead-drifting" downstream. Even if he does, it's questionable whether he takes it for a minnow or perhaps a large nymph. Usually the strike will come when the line is tight, with some movement being imparted by the current, by the angler, or both.

Most streamer fishermen use several different methods to impart motion to the fly in an attempt to make it move like a living creature: making short, quick pulls on the line as it is stripped in; making longer, smoother movements of the rod tip, followed by letting the fly drift back downstream a little; or stripping in the line in rather long, quick movements, interspersed with pauses. In water of differing speeds, you will need to employ different techniques to get a lifelike movement from your streamer, and each of the above methods will work at times. In most cases, then, I would cast the fly upstream and follow its downstream movement with the rod tip. At a point approximately opposite our position, the slack will come out of the line, and from this point until the fly makes its swing back across the current,

I am in direct control of its movement. If I have judged my cast properly, the fly will make the swing across current when it is at the right depth and in the right position for presentation in the target lie. When the fly stops directly downstream below me, I let it pause there for a moment because often a trout will have followed it as it made its swing across stream and is just ready to strike at that moment. I generally let it hang there for a few seconds and then give it a couple of quick, short twitches, letting it fall back into position. If there is a trout that has followed the streamer, he is almost certain to strike when the "minnow" is suddenly getting away. If I don't get a strike after a couple of short, quick movements there, then I work the fly upstream towards me, using one of the movements we described earlier. People have written books devoted entirely to streamer fishing. What we have provided here is just a beginning, but a sound one. The most important thing to keep in mind is that you are imitating a minnow with your fly, and you must handle it so that its movements will appear as natural as those of a real little fish.

WADING
THE STREAM

To get into the best position in order to get optimum presentation of the fly requires the ability to wade the stream quietly and safely. There are many factors that affect the manner in which we wade a particular stretch of water. Bottom type, water speed, water depth, and even water clarity should all be taken into consideration when wading. Unfortunately, this aspect of fly-fishing doesn't get the attention it should because anglers are so intent on the act of fishing. Not only does this inattention often lead to a bath, it causes us to fish less effectively.

A primary reason that the fly fisher needs to be able to wade is to provide enough room for the backcast. Many trout streams are surrounded by trees, brush, or terrain that is simply not conducive to standing on the edge to cast. To achieve the needed clearance for the line, move into the stream where you can direct the cast parallel to the water's flow.

Another important reason to wade is so you can cross the stream to fish both bank edges. On a typical winding meadow stream, you are basically limited to fishing only one half of the stream if you stay on one bank. As the stream winds back and forth, the deeper, fish-holding undercut banks alternate with each turn, and in order to be able to cover all the productive lies, you must be able to move freely across the stream.

The most important reason for wading, though, is to be able to move into a position that will enable you to present the fly to the trout in the best possible manner with the least effort. We are all guilty of repeatedly casting too far, fighting a really difficult drift situation, or working too hard to control the line on the water, when we could remedy all of the problems by simply taking a few moments to better our casting position. Let's take a look at some of the factors that affect wading.

Bottom Type

The type of stream bottom, first of all, dictates the type of soles you need on your waders or wading shoes. Cleated rubber soles provide sure footing in mud, sand, or other soft bottom material. They are treacherous, however, when wading streams with rocky bottoms because the wet rubber is very slippery. Felt soles, on the other hand, grip firmly on moss-covered rocks, a fact that you simply can't believe until you've experienced it. But felt soles quickly become skis in mud or silt and are horrible on wet grass that grows along the bank, or worse yet, on frost-covered surfaces. About the best you can do is to buy waders with the type of sole that works best where you spend most of your time fishing—and be careful when fishing other bottom types.

Bottom structure also dictates how you wade a particular section of stream. A sand or mud bottom usually doesn't have a lot of obstructions, and you can wade securely, concentrating only on depth and force of the current. The simple fact that there aren't many obstructions constitutes a trap, though. Just when you become accustomed to the freedom of movement pro-

vided by the smooth bottom, you discover the one and only rock in the whole pool, or the log lying on the bottom. The Miracle Mile section of the North Platte in Wyoming gets me several times each trip.

Our favorite stretch is on the edge of an island just above a reservoir. Big browns settle in to spawn in this stretch in late fall. There is a smooth bank about 6 or 8 feet wide between the sharp cut of the island and the river, which means that you need to wade out 5 or 6 feet into the river to get room for a backcast. The browns that we are after aren't resident fish; they are monsters (some over 20 pounds) that come out of the lake to spawn. The river flow is very strong, and when you hook into a good fish you have to move downstream with him or he's going to quickly take all your line and backing and break off. The bottom is relatively smooth along the edge—just a few softball-size rocks—and you quickly get used to being able to move easily in the knee-deep water. There's a submerged log about halfway down to the rapids at the end of the island, whose middle section is raised about a foot off the bottom, just about ankle high.

I'm sure you can envision the scenario. You hook a large fish and shuffle downstream as fast as you can in the knee-deep water to keep him from running out your line and backing. You watch the fish as he jumps, trying to keep as much pressure on him as possible and trying to keep the line from getting tangled in the large rocks out in the river. Just as the trout gets dangerously close to the head of the rapids, you start gaining on him and getting some of your line back. Now you start sloshing along as fast as you possibly can and, ouch! Your foot slides under the log and over you go, headfirst into the river. It doesn't happen often, but often enough for that log to be officially christened "gotcha." Unofficially, it has been christened with just about every other name you have ever heard, and they are not limited to those found in your Funk & Wagnalls.

Even stream sections with smooth bottoms and few obstructions often have thick weeds. They can accumulate around your ankles as you wade, and, before long, you will be stepping on them like untied shoelaces, and down you go.

Very soft bottoms present another hazard: you sink into them. Finding yourself suddenly trapped in the bottom of a stream, unable to move your feet, is a frightening experience! The best way out is to pull one foot upwards and wiggle it back and forth, shift your weight to that foot, then pull up and wiggle the other foot, and so on, until you can get one of them free. These situations are caused either by moving too fast into the area or by standing too long in one spot, not noticing that you were slowly sinking. In an area with a soft bottom, move slowly, making sure you can extract your foot before applying your full weight to it. Also, while standing, keep moving your feet slightly to keep them free, and if you find that they are sinking as you move them, back out of the spot.

Our Western streams are typically strewn with moss-covered rocks that range in size from a cantaloupe to a house. I haven't fallen over the house-size ones yet, but the smaller ones are treacherous, because in addition to being slippery, they are often stacked on top of each other and can move suddenly when you step on them. Wading in this type of water is best done by shuffling your feet slowly so that you don't take a step and find that your foot is under the edge of a rock, throwing you off balance. You also learn

very quickly to shift your weight slowly to your foot to make sure the rock won't move. I have seen some incredible rock-hopping sequences by my fishing companions. I watched Steve traverse a hundred yards or so along the edge of the Arkansas River with only the aid of six or eight momentary touches to intervening rocks. This particular trek ended harmlessly when he finally reached a shallow section of the stream where he could regain his balance. I've executed some gymnastic ballet myself in an effort to avoid falling, only to keep gaining momentum so that the finale was a grand splash. Such gyrations are not only foolish, they can be very dangerous.

If you find that you have lost your balance and are headed for a dunking, the best thing you can do is accept the inevitable—sit down. Sure, you're going to get wet, but odds are you're going to end up falling anyway. The mad dance from unstable rock to unstable rock, with equipment flying everywhere, only serves to make the ending harder and more likely to lead to injury, to you and your equipment.

Water Speed and Depth

Both the speed and depth of the water should influence your wading judgment. In sections of most streams you can safely wade as deeply as your waders allow, but in other sections of the same stream you would be foolish to get in above your ankles. The section of the Miracle Mile that I mentioned earlier is a good example. In the stretch where we fish, the bottom slopes from the shore along the island to a depth of about 12 feet or so. The slope is gradual, and, if it weren't for the force of the water, we could probably wade 20 or 30 feet out from shore. Although the water is unbroken (because of the depth), the current is very strong, and only a fool would wade out more than about hip deep. When standing out about thigh deep, we can feel the sand washing out from under our feet. Yet, we invariably see anglers wade out where they are slowly bobbed downstream by the current. No fish, not even a 20-pound brown, is worth risking your life for; a consideration apparently overlooked by those waders.

When wading streams that are deep and swift, take along a wading staff, which serves several purposes: to probe ahead of where you wade to make sure you don't step into a hole, to provide a firm means of regaining lost balance, and to ensure at least two anchor points on the bottom at all times. Older anglers in particular should consider carrying a staff to help them negotiate a stream. There are a couple of collapsible models on the market that are easy to carry, and they will serve well for those unexpected occasions when a staff would be helpful. But for those places that we know are treacherous, we take a really strong staff that Don made.

He bored a hole in the end of a push-broom handle and epoxied a 1/2-inch piece of steel rod into the hole. He attached a 3- or 4-foot section of parachute cord through a hole in the top of the handle to be attached to the wading vest. When wading I hold it in my hand, and when fishing I let it float along at the end of the cord so it is out of the way and still readily available. It's not the kind of thing that you would want to carry along on all your trips, but when you head for big, fast water, it's just the ticket, quickly available and sturdy enough to instill confidence. Sure is "mud ugly," though. If you are caught without a wading staff when you need one, look around the stream.

Sticks and branches on the ground can suffice to help you across a section of heavy flow. Test one before you plunge in, though. You don't want to find that it has a weak spot and have it break just when you need it the most.

The safest and easiest water to cross is usually above knee deep. Water shallower than that is usually very swift and difficult to gain a footing in. Unless the water flow is very weak, don't try to wade directly up- or downstream when the full width of your body counters the force of the water. Instead, angle across the flow.

Wading upstream is very tiring but is safer than moving with the water's flow. Moving downstream, with the water at your back, can quickly develop into the same problem as starting to run downhill: you keep going faster and faster until you can't keep your balance any longer. If this happens, about the only thing you can do is angle towards the shallower water along the shore. If you continue to lose your balance, bounce off the bottom. With each bounce, the water will carry you farther downstream, and if you are headed towards the shore, you will eventually be pushed into shallower water where you can regain your balance.

The most precarious time when wading is when you need to turn around. Perhaps you've angled upstream to a casting position and need to angle back downstream to get back to shore. When you start to turn around, you are going to present a lot more body area to the force of the water, and it's easy to get thrown off balance. The trick is to lean slightly into the current by bending your knees and then exaggerating that lean as more and more of your body is exposed to the current. This is one place where a wading staff is a great help.

Water Clarity

It's just plain easier to wade when you can see the bottom! Even heavy water can be negotiated if you can see the bottom, avoid obstacles, and see where the little quiet spaces are behind the rocks. Polarized glasses are helpful. In water where you can't see beneath the surface, you simply must wade more slowly and carefully, making sure of your footing before shifting your weight to that foot.

As fly fishers, we accept wading as an integral part of the sport and, like casting, don't even think about it most of the time. Every year several of our fellow anglers drown while fishing, either because they weren't being careful or were tempted beyond the limits of good judgment. A fall into shallow water can easily lead to a broken wrist or arm, and if you hit your head, you could easily be knocked unconscious and drown.

A fall in deep water requires all the strength you can muster to avoid disaster. If you should find yourself being carried downstream, roll over on your back and get your legs downstream so you can push away from any boulders or other obstructions. Forget about your equipment—you're in serious trouble and your life is worth more than even that brand new rod and reel. You must remain calm; panic will only make things worse. If you stay calm and concentrate on keeping afloat, the stream will carry you along, and you will eventually be swept into shallower water where you can halt your downstream journey or where you can get hold of a rock or branch along the stream's edge and extricate yourself. The same principles that apply to wading safely also ensure that you wade successfully—not putting down the fish by excessive rock rolling and splashing. Wade slowly, feeling your way with each step until you are in position to start casting. Take your time wading, think about where you are going, and don't be so anxious to catch a fish that your judgment is impaired.

Oh, and don't worry about your waders filling up and dragging you to the bottom. First of all, wear a wading belt so they won't fill up but, even if they do, the weight of the water inside is the same as outside the waders . . . neutral buoyancy. When you go to get out of the river, however, things change drastically, your waders suddenly weigh a lot more than you are used to, and getting up can be a problem. The best solution is to wade carefully and don't fall in. Barring that, wear a wading belt!

STREAM ETIQUETTE

Fly fishers have, historically, been members of the upper classes because only they had access to streams. That history is the sport's blessing—and its curse. Because these early practitioners were from cultured backgrounds, fly-fishing evolved into a gentle, contemplative pursuit. Men, and later, women, acted in gentlemanly and ladylike fashion on the stream. Mannerly conduct has always been a part of fly-fishing and one of its real joys at present. Unfortunately, the sport has also suffered because many thought it was only for those who wear ascots. It was assumed (and sometimes implied) that somehow fly-fishing was simply beyond the means and the understanding of us common folk. Some of that stigma still remains, and we are constantly reminded of it when interested people often inquire whether they are capable of learning to fly-fish. Sometimes we even detect a note of concern about their "worthiness" to pursue such a lofty goal. It all needs to be put into perspective.

As we wrote in the Introduction, fly-fishing transcends the boundaries of age, status, or wealth. It isn't so difficult that anyone with reasonable intelligence and hand and eye coordination can't become proficient. On the other hand, fly-fishing isn't just another method of catching fish. It is more involved and requires more from the angler. To be a successful, complete fly fisher, you must expend time and effort to understand the trout, its behavior, and its environment. Then you will see that there is a heritage behind all that we do, a heritage that is worth preserving because it is what makes fly-fishing unique.

Our stream manner is the outward expression of that heritage and not only makes the sport more enjoyable for all of us, but serves to keep it the gentle sport that it is. Stream etiquette isn't unique to those of us who fish with a fly. I have often shared a section of stream with spinner fishermen and bait fishermen who displayed good manners. Neither is stream etiquette universal among fly fishers; unfortunately, we can count some real slobs among our numbers. And there isn't much difference between the slob and the snob; both represent our sport in its worst possible light. The rules of stream etiquette are nothing more than good common sense. But since they may entail things that the beginner might not think of, we'll go over them so you will feel more comfortable on the stream.

Two's a Crowd

First of all, you should never crowd another angler. The temptation is sometimes very strong to fish the same water as those who are catching a lot of fish, but that is just as rude as cutting in on the serving line at a restaurant. Let's say you come up to a pool where a fly fisher is catching fish, or maybe it just looks like a good pool, but someone is already there. Most of us would stop well back from the edge so the fish wouldn't stop feeding, and watch for a while. For one thing, fly-fishing is a beautiful sport to watch, and, of course, we might learn something.

If it is a large pool, there is nothing wrong with quietly entering the water where the first person has already fished or going well beyond the angler and into a fresh section. If the pool isn't large, you should go on to the next section that you find fishable. I have often spent a pleasant day leapfrogging from pool to pool with a fly fisher whom I didn't know, watching him for a while as I passed "his" pools, and he watching me as he moved on ahead.

There is a delightful exception to the "two's a crowd" point. Some of the most enjoyable days we've had on the river were when we have fished with another person, taking turns. The game we play is that you fish until either: (1) you take a fish, or (2) you miss a fish and then it's my turn. Wow, do you ever learn a lot watching another fly fisher from close up and, besides, you get a break from wading all the time. Needless to say, this doesn't work with all personalities, and the "guerilla" fly fishers won't be able to stand the waiting until it's their turn to attack the river again. With the right companion, though, it can make for a very special day of fishing.

Be Friendly

All fly fishers have a common bond and should have an appreciation for the other members. If you meet another angler out of the stream, take a moment to share your experiences of the day. Maybe you can shed some light on the patterns that are working and contribute to his having a good day, or maybe he will share some insight he has gained that will improve your success. A nod of the head or a wave of the hand will serve as both a greeting and an acknowledg-

9-1. Paul and Don on their beloved Arkansas River in Colorado.

ment of the other's presence, if one of you is in the stream.

My son, Mace, and I were fishing the Elk River one year and had been having a banner day. We had caught and released dozens of fish and had decided to drive to another spot on the river when we met another fly fisher coming along the bank. He was friendly, and when I asked how he had been doing he said that he had taken two or three fish but things seemed to be slow today. I asked what fly he had been using, thinking that I would share our experience with him. He responded that he would rather not say. I then noticed that he had his fly cupped in his hand so that we couldn't see it. I suppose that I should have been more charitable, but his selfishness ticked me off. So I decided not to mention what we had found to be the best pattern. We watched him for a while before we drove off, and, although he cast well and fished all the right places, we didn't see him take a fish.

I've never understood why some anglers are afraid of sharing. Are they concerned that I'm going to catch all the fish and leave none for them? Do they somehow feel that the less successful others are, the more important their success becomes? Most of us delight in being able to help others by offering suggestions on what patterns and techniques work. Be one of us; we catch more fish and have more fun.

Perhaps more important than being friendly to other fly fishers is being friendly towards other anglers who aren't using flies. You may never know that the few minutes you spent talking with the non-fly fisher and explaining a little about your equipment and the sport resulted in their conversion. But that's how many of us got started.

Respect the Environment

Take care of the environment. The areas where we fly fishers spend our time are so beautiful; let's keep them that way. Don't ever litter. I know many fly fishers who think nothing of picking up what litter they do find and carrying it out with them. It only takes a moment and will serve to keep the area as pretty as you've come to expect it.

Respect the Trout

The trout is a noble and worthy quarry, one which nature has blessed with temperament and instinct that make him a real challenge. Let's preserve him! Many areas of the country now have restrictive laws regarding limits, and it goes without saying that the fly fisher must adhere to those laws. If you truly enjoy pursuing trout, though, why take any fish? They are a renewable resource, but, more important, they are a preservable resource. By returning the trout to the stream, you are assured of continuing fishing pleasure, for yourself, and for your sons and daughters. As you can see, the basics of stream etiquette are very simple. Be considerate of your fellow fishermen, and you'll always be a welcome stream companion.

■ APPENDIXES

Selected Fly Patterns

CHOOSING ONE FLY PATTERN from the tens of thousands that are available can easily confuse the beginner. Keep in mind, though, our discussions about the food forms that trout feed upon.

Most fly patterns are meant to represent different stages of common aquatic insects or of minnows that might be present in a stream. There are thousands of methods, techniques, and materials that the fly-tyer can use to arrive at an imitation that duplicates the silhouette, size, and color of a particular food form. That latitude in tying technique, materials, and methods has resulted in hundreds of different patterns that may imitate the same food form.

Any dry fly whose wings are tied upright simply must be a mayfly imitation, because mayflies are the only aquatic insects that carry their wings in that position. An imitation with wings tied down over the back may look like either a caddisfly or a stonefly to the trout. A pattern tied with the wings spread out to the sides might be taken by the trout as either a midge or spent-wing mayfly; size and color would be the determining factor in the latter two cases. See the patterns on pages 122 through 127 in this appendix.

Mayfly and stonefly nymphs can both be imitated with the same patterns, again with size and color better imitating one insect or the other. Caddis larvae and midge larvae resemble each other closely in silhouette and, in some cases, even in size and color. If you were to ask 10 different accomplished tyers to tie a fly to represent a given food form, you would probably get six or seven different patterns. What it all amounts to is that the name given to a fly is irrelevant; if it looks like the food form that the trout is feeding upon, it will work.

All of this, then, makes it very difficult to recommend certain flies, particularly when so many patterns are regional. What we have tried to do is supply a list of patterns that are good imitations of the major food forms and are readily available throughout the country. Certainly, if particular patterns are commonly used in your area and are not on our list, don't hesitate to use them! They are most likely patterns that have developed regionally and, therefore, will be very effective in that area, which brings us to another important point. If you are serious about getting involved in fly-fishing, you should learn to tie your own flies.

The first advantage is the money you can save. Nowadays quality flies are around two dollars each, and some of the more complex patterns cost more than three dollars. More important, though, are the other advantages.

In order to tie your own flies, you must develop a better understanding of the trout's feeding habits, the food forms available to them, and the stream habitat. That knowledge is sure to make your fishing ventures more rewarding, both in the number of fish you take and in your appreciation of the environment.

If you can tie your own flies, you can tie what you need, when you need it. Some days would have been much less successful if we had not been capable of tying some flies while on the stream. Tying ability comes in handy when we simply don't have the right flies with us, or when we have only a limited number and run out.

A good example is when we fish the Miracle Mile in Wyoming. The stretch of river that we fish is about 25 miles from the nearest place to buy flies, and because of the river's characteristics and the type of fishing required, it's easy to lose a dozen streamers a day. We usually go up for five days of fishing, which might mean that we use as many as 60 flies each. At $2.00 apiece, that would amount to $120 just in flies! Worse yet is if you run out and then have to go find and buy even more flies, losing half a day of fishing in the process.

Another advantage to tying your own flies is that you don't have to worry about losing them. If you lay out hard cash for flies, you're going to be rather careful about where you attempt to cast. Consequently, you will miss a lot of good fish (often the biggest in the river) because you can't afford to risk three or four flies to cast back under that bush or over that log to get the fly to the fish.

The best reason for tying your own flies is really simple: it's fun! All the advantages mentioned above are good justifications for taking up fly-tying, but the pleasure derived from tying is reason enough.

◾ Dry Flies

Renegade

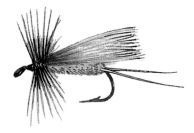

Elk-hair Caddis

Olive Quill

Ant

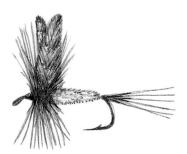

Irresistible

Adams

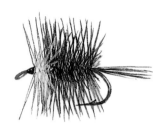

Bivisible

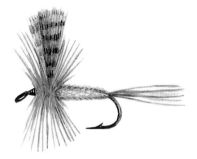

Light Cahill

Sofa Pillow

Humpy

Grasshopper

Royal Wulff

■ Nymphs

Hare's Ear

Miracle Nymph

Brassie

Muskrat

Peeping Caddis

March Brown

Sparkle Pupa

Zug Bug

Woolly Worm

Montana Nymph

Light Stone

Dark Stone

■ Streamers

Little Rainbow Trout

Spruce Fly

Muddler Minnow

Little Brown Trout

Platte River Special

Dace

Marabou

Black/yellow Matuka

Olive Matuka

Hornberg

Zonker

Spuddler

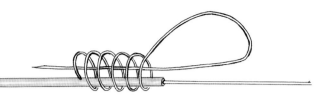

KNOTS

WE THOUGHT IT WOULD BE BENEFICIAL TO SHOW in condensed form the instructions for tying all the knots that the fly fisher needs to be able to tie. That way, you don't need to search them out in the text.

▦ Nail Knot: For joining fly line to backing and leader to fly line.

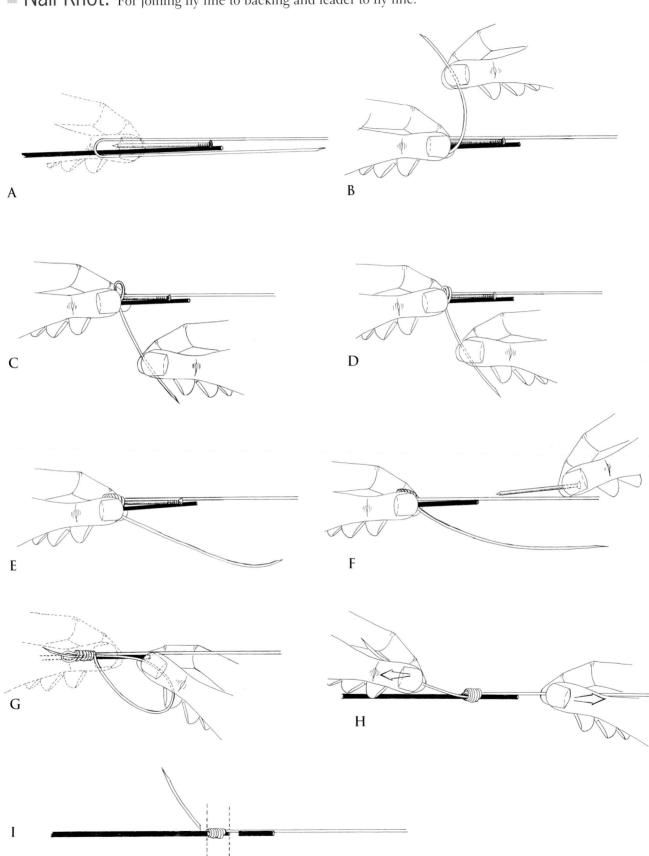

A

B

C

D

E

F

G

H

I

■ Needle Knot: An improved method of attaching leader to fly line.

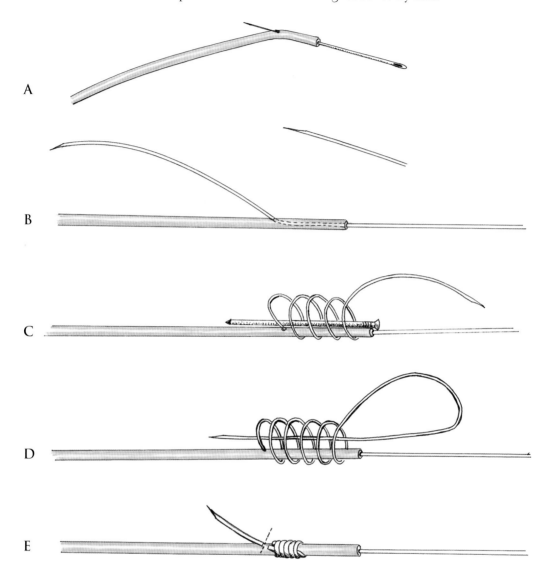

A

B

C

D

E

■ Epoxy Slice: Another method of joining leader to fly line.

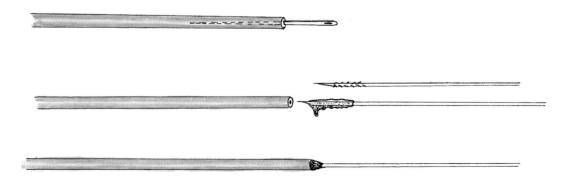

Blood Knot: For tying sections of leader material together. Works only with leader material sections of approximately the same size (2X or smaller difference in size).

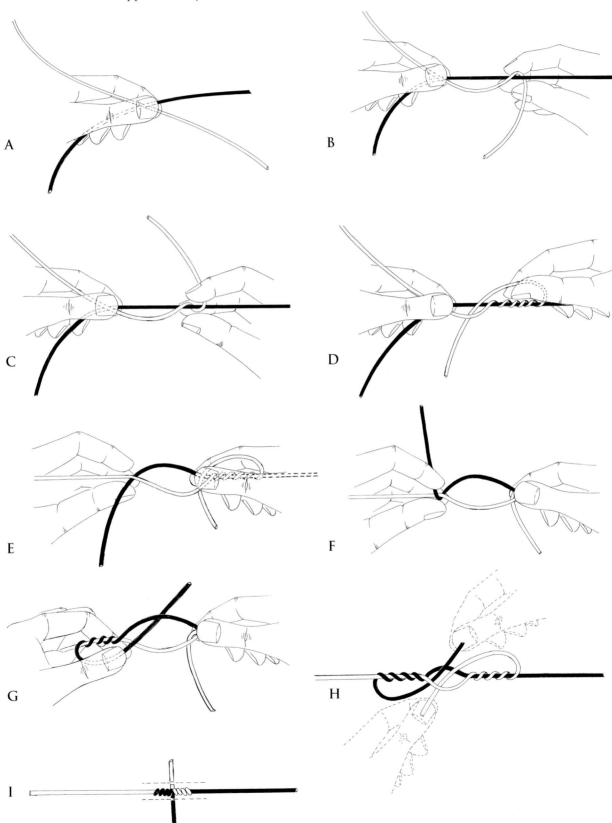

Surgeon's Knot: For tying sections of leader material together, but will work with materials of greatly unequal diameters.

A

B

C

D

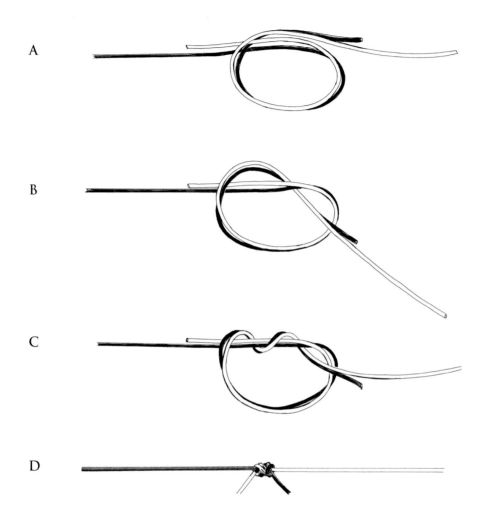

Clinch Knot: A common knot for tying the fly to the leader.

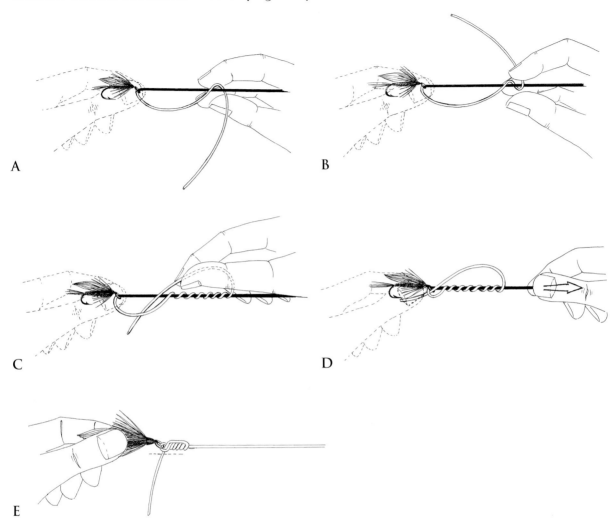

A

B

C

D

E

Improved Clinch Knot: A better knot for attaching the fly to the leader.

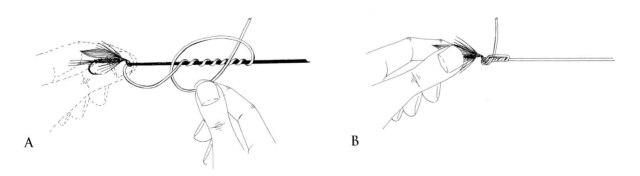

A

B

▧ Trilene Knot: Another version of the clinch knot with improved knot strength.

A

B

C

D

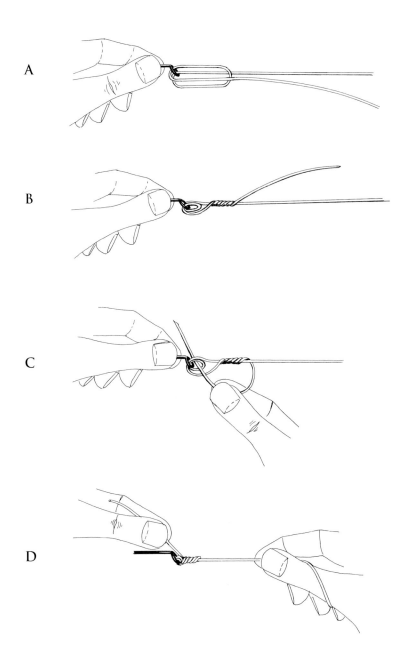

COMMON TROUT SPECIES

RAINBOW TROUT

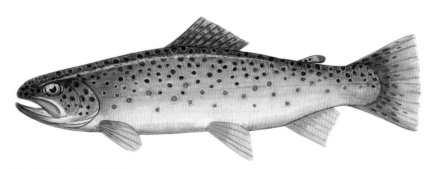

BROWN TROUT

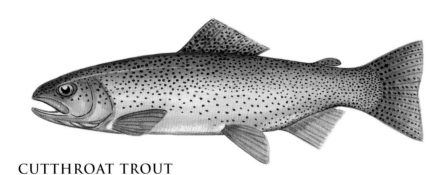

CUTTHROAT TROUT

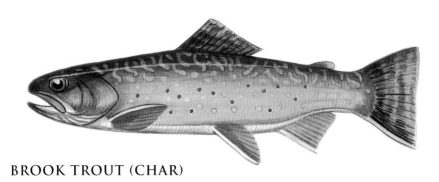

BROOK TROUT (CHAR)

GLOSSARY

FLY-FISHING HAS A VOCABULARY OF ITS OWN, which includes common words with uncommon meanings and words that are unique to the pursuit. Since a comprehensive glossary would be as long as a dictionary, we have selected those terms that you will encounter when first taking up the sport. Most of the terms are mentioned in this book, but we have also chosen some related words. We hope you will use this glossary not only as a reference but also for a quick read-through to familiarize yourself with the terms before plunging into Chapter 1.

across-stream: Perpendicular to the flow of the stream.

action: A general term often used in an attempt to describe the feel of a rod (soft, slow, hard, or fast action).

adult: The mature stage in the life cycle of an insect.

alderfly: A member of the order Megaloptera; complete metamorphosis.

artificial: A type of fly made to imitate the living insect.

attractor: A fly that is not tied so that it imitates a particular food form, usually bright-colored.

automatic reel: A fly reel in which a spring is wound as line is stripped; the action of the spring is then used to retrieve the line.

backcast: That portion of the fly cast in which the line moves towards the area behind the angler.

backing line: Usually braided nylon or Dacron that is tied between the reel spool and the fly line, used to help fill the spool, to attach the fly line to the spool, and to provide an extra length of line for fighting the fish.

baitfish: Any one of the small fish or minnows that are eaten by the trout.

balance: The proper combination of line, rod, and reel that results in an efficient, effective system for fly-fishing.

bamboo: A tropical grass (Tonkin cane) whose stem is used in the construction of fly rods.

barb: The nick cut out of the point of a hook, so that once the hook penetrates, it won't return through the puncture.

barbless hook: A hook made without a barb, or a hook on which the barb has been removed or flattened.

barrel knot: Another name for the blood knot, used for joining two pieces of monofilament of nearly equal diameters.

beetle: A common name for members of the order Coleoptera; there are both aquatic and terrestrial beetles that may be important to the fly fisher.

belly: The sagging portion of a fly line, whether in the air or on the stream.

belly boat: Another term for a float tube, a belly boat consists of a fabric seat, attached to a large inner tube, on which the angler sits so he can float on the surface of the water.

bend: The curved section at the rear of a hook.

blank: A rod without handle, reel seat, or guides.

blood knot: Common name for the barrel knot; used for joining two pieces of monofilament of nearly equal diameters, particularly sections of leader material.

boron: A metalloid element used in the manufacture of fly rods.

brook trout (Salvelinus fontinalis): A member of the Salmonidae family but a char, not a true trout. Commonly referred to as brook trout, however.

brown trout (Salmo trutta): A true trout and one of the fly fisher's favorite quarries.

bucktail: A type of streamer fly, so named because the wing is typically tied using hair from the tail of a white-tailed deer.

caddis: A member of the order Trichoptera; undergoes complete metamorphosis. The caddis (or caddisfly) is one of the most important insects in the diet of most trout and, therefore, is of great importance to the fly fisherman.

cane: Another name for bamboo, a tropical grass whose stem is used in the construction of fly rods.

cased caddis: Any of the caddis that build a case in which to live during the larval stage.

cast: The act of using the rod to impart energy into the fly line so that the line (and attached leader and fly) is thrown some distance away from the angler; also, two or more flies attached on the same leader for presentation to the trout (a cast of flies).

chest waders: Waterproof waders that come up nearly to the armpits of the wearer.

clinch knot: A knot commonly used for tying the fly to the leader tippet.

clinch knot (improved): Same as the clinch knot, but the tag end is turned back through the knot before tightening to prevent the knot from slipping.

Coleoptera: The order of insects that includes all beetles; undergoes complete metamorphosis.

complete metamorphosis: An insect's life cycle, which includes four distinct stages—egg, larva, pupa, and adult.

complex hatch: The simultaneous hatching of several types and/or species of insects.

compound hatch: The masking, or hiding, of a hatch of smaller insects by a hatch of larger insects, which occurs at the same time.

cork: Material used for most fly rod handles; term is also sometimes used in lieu of handle.

crane fly: An insect of the order Diptera that resembles a large mosquito in the adult stage. Some species are terrestrial and some are aquatic. They undergo complete metamorphosis.

curve cast: A fly cast in which the angler makes the leader and fly move in a perpendicular direction to that of the cast.

cutthroat trout (*Oncorhynchus clarki*): true trout found mostly in the western United States.

damselfly: A large aquatic insect of the order Odonata, suborder Zygoptera, that resembles its close relative the dragonfly.

dapping: A fishing technique in which the fly is repeatedly bounced on and off the water's surface.

dead drift: A method of presenting the fly in which no motion is imparted by the angler.

Diptera: The order of insects, commonly called midges, which contains the true flies. Dipterans have two wings and undergo complete metamorphosis.

dobsonfly: Members of the order Megaloptera; complete metamorphosis; large insects whose larvae are commonly called hellgrammites.

Dolly Varden (*Salvelinus malma*): A char, although usually called Dolly Varden trout; may actually be a subspecies of the Arctic char.

double-haul: A casting stroke in which additional force is imparted to the rod at the beginning of both the forward cast and backward cast by sharply pulling the line with the line hand.

double-tapered line: A fly line that is heaviest in the center and tapers equally towards each end.

down-eye hook: A hook with the eye bent below the shank.

downstream: In the direction of the stream's flow.

drag: The force of the water against a line or leader, which causes the fly to move unnaturally in or on the water; also the mechanical system in a reel that applies friction to the spool.

dragonfly: A large aquatic insect of the order Odonata, suborder Anisoptera, which resembles its close relative the damsel fly; undergoes incomplete metamorphosis.

drake: A common term for the adult male mayfly.

dropper: The secondary fly attached to the leader in a cast of flies.

dry fly: A fly that is tied to represent the adult stage of an insect and designed to float on the water's surface.

dun: A common term for the subimago, or first winged stage, of the adult mayfly.

emerger: A term used loosely to describe any insect that moves up towards the water's surface preparatory to hatching into the adult stage.

entomology: The formal study of insects.

Ephemeroptera: The order of insects containing the mayflies; incomplete metamorphosis but unique in that they have two adult stages: subimago (dun) and imago (spinner).

eye: The loop formed at the forward end of a hook to which the tippet is attached.

false cast: A casting stroke in which the line is kept moving; used to dry the fly, to work out line, and to adjust line length.

feeding: The active taking of food by fish.

feeding lane: The narrow strip of current that carries food to the trout's feeding lie.

feeding lie: A position in the stream where trout go to actively feed.

felt soles: A surface applied to the bottoms of hip boots, waders, or wading shoes to provide traction on moss- or algae-covered rocks; originally only wool felt was used, but manmade materials are now common.

ferrule: Originally the male and female metal pieces that connect two sections of a rod, now used to refer to the connection itself, even if one rod section fits into the other without metal connectors.

fiberglass: A common rod material consisting of glass fibers extending the length of the rod section.

flat water: Unbroken water surface.

float: The action of a dry fly on the water (a drag-free float, a long float, etc.).

floatant: A substance applied to a line, fly, or leader to assist it in floating.

floating line: A fly line designed and built to float.

float tube: A fabric seat attached to an inner tube, which enables the angler to float on the surface of the water; also called a belly boat.

fly: An arrangement of materials on a hook which are meant to entice a fish to bite.

fly box: A container designed specifically for storing flies.

forceps: A small, pliers-like tool that locks closed; it assists the fly fisherman in holding small items or in removing a fly from the fish.

forward cast: That portion of a fly cast in which the line moves towards the front of the caster.

free-living caddis: Caddis species that don't build permanent cases during the larval stage.

freestone streams: Tumbling, fast-moving streams, usually with rock-covered bottoms. They are subject to great changes in depth and speed because they are formed from an accumulation of trickles from small springs, snowmelt, or rainfall, which originate at high elevations.

free-swimming caddis: Same as free-living caddis.

French snap: A small clamp, often used by the fly fisherman to attach his net to his vest. The snap is normally in the closed position and is opened by squeezing the sides.

glass: A slang term for fiberglass.

golden trout (Oncorhynchus aguabonita): A beautiful trout native only to the Mt. Whitney area in California; has been transplanted but is normally found only at elevations above 8,000 feet.

grannom: A common term for a caddisfly.

graphite: A mineral and also a manmade material, consisting of carbon fibers. Synthetic graphite is used in the manufacture of strong, lightweight fly rods.

grayling (Thymallus arcticus): Not a true trout or char but a member of the salmonid family, characterized by its large, brightly colored dorsal fin.

greased: Treated with floatant.

grip: The handle of the rod; also, the hand position used in holding the rod.

guides: The devices on the rod through which the line runs.

hair-winged: Having wings made of hair, as in a hair-winged dry fly.

hand retrieve: Retrieval technique in which the line is alternately picked up between the thumb and forefinger and then between the thumb and little finger.

hatch: The transformation of an insect into its adult form; also, the emergence of a large number of adults at one time (a hatch of insects).

hen: A female insect; normally used in reference to mayflies.

high-density line: A sinking fly line built in such a way that its density is much greater than that of water so that it sinks very fast.

hip boots: Waterproof boots with tops that come to the wearer's upper thighs.

hippers: Another name for hip boots.

holding lie: Where a trout normally remains when not actively feeding.

hook keeper: A small hook mounted onto a fly rod, just forward of the handle, where the fly can be hooked when not in use.

imitation: A fly tied to represent realistically a particular food form—as opposed to an attractor.

incomplete metamorphosis: An insect's life cycle that includes only three stages—egg, nymph, and adult.

instar: A stage in the life cycle of an insect between two successive molts.

jassid: A common name for a leaf hopper; also, a fly pattern meant to imitate the Japanese beetle.

keel fly: A fly tied on a hook that has an additional bend on the shank so that the fly will lie in or on the water with the point of the hook turned up, making the fly nearly weedless.

knotted leader: A leader made by tying together lengths of monofilament of decreasing diameter to achieve a taper.

knotless leader: A leader whose taper is formed in the manufacturing process instead of by the angler's graduating the leader from large to small by tying together several sizes of monofilament.

larva: The stage between the egg and pupa in the life cycle of an insect undergoing complete metamorphosis; characterized by a wormlike appearance.

leader: A section of monofilament line, usually tapered, that is attached to the end of the fly line and to which the fly is tied.

leader sink: Any of several materials used to treat a leader so that it will break the surface tension and sink below the surface of the water.

leader straightener: A double-sided pad, usually lined with rubber, through which the leader is drawn to take out any kinks.

leader wheel: A colloquial term for tippet material, derived from the small spools or wheels that tippet material comes wound on.

leeches: Carnivorous or bloodsucking annelid worms that inhabit most lakes; common trout food.

Leisenring lift: A technique used in nymph fishing where the line is lifted, causing the imitation fly to move upwards, just in front of a trout's suspected lie.

level line: A fly line with the same diameter from end to end.

lie: A particular spot where a trout may be found (a holding lie, a feeding lie, a resting lie).

life cycle: The stages in the development of an insect from egg to adult.

line hand: The hand that does not hold the fly rod when casting.

line weight: A designation of the weight of a fly line, which is actually based on the weight of the first 30 feet.

loop: The candy-cane shape that a fly line takes during the casting stroke.

loop control: The manner in which the shape of the loop is formed during the cast. Loop control is the essence of fly casting.

marabou streamer: A streamer fly tied using marabou feathers as the wings.

masking hatch: The emergence of adult aquatic insects in which a large, brightly colored species hides a smaller species.

mayfly: An aquatic insect of the order Ephemeroptera; one of the primary food sources for trout.

mend: The act of controlling the fly line on the water; usually the motion of flipping the belly of the line back upstream.

metamorphosis: A series of changes in the physical form of an insect. Complete metamorphosis includes egg, larval, pupal, and adult stages; incomplete metamorphosis includes egg, nymphal, and adult stages only.

microcaddis: Any of several species of caddisflies that are very small.

midge: The common name for members of the order Diptera; also, any small insect or small artificial.

midge rod: A short, lightweight fly rod.

mosquito: Member of the order Diptera, family Culicidae.

nail knot: The most common knot for attaching the butt of the leader to the fly line.

natural: A living insect, as opposed to an artificial, or manmade, insect or fly.

needle knot: A common knot used for attaching the butt of the leader to the fly line.

net: A piece of equipment consisting of a frame with an open-weave conical bag attached, used to land a hooked fish; also called a landing net.

nippers: Another term for clippers, used to closely trim the tag ends of line after knots are tied.

no-hackle fly: A type of dry fly, popularized by Swisher and Richards, which doesn't use hackle as the support for the floating fly.

no-kill: A rule (sometimes an individual's philosophy) whereby all fish that are caught are returned to the water unharmed.

nymph: The stage between the egg and the adult in the life cycle of an insect that undergoes an incomplete metamorphosis; also any artificial that is imitative of any underwater stage of various insects; e.g., even though a caddisfly does not go through a nymphal stage, the flies that imitate this insect's underwater forms are often referred to as nymphs.

nymphing: Any of various fishing techniques in which the angler presents an imitation of an underwater stage of an insect.

Odonata: An order of insects containing the dragonflies and damsel flies; undergoes incomplete metamorphosis.

Oncorhynchus aguabonita: The Latin name for golden trout.

Oncorhynchus clarki: The Latin name for cutthroat trout.

Oncorhynchus mykiss: The Latin name for rainbow trout.

oviposit: The act of laying eggs, particularly among insects.

periwinkle: A colloquial term for cased caddis larva or pupa.

Plecoptera: The order of insects containing the stone flies; incomplete metamorphosis.

pocket water: A water type in which the surface is mostly broken but does contain some small areas (or pockets) of smooth water.

poly-wing: A dry fly tied with polypropylene yarn for the wings.

pool: A relatively smooth, unbroken water surface. Generally, the pools in a stream may be the most obvious fishing areas, but they are not always the most productive.

presentation: The method of placing a fly where a fish will most likely see it; includes the manner in which the cast is completed and the method in which the fly is fished.

pupa: The stage between the larva and adult in the life cycle of an insect.

rainbow trout (Oncorhynchus mykiss): A true trout and one of the species most sought after by the fly fisher.

reach cast: A line-presentation method in which the rod is moved left or right at the completion of the cast, before it falls to the water. This method is used to move the belly of the line upstream to increase the length of the drag-free drift achieved.

reel seat: The mechanism on a rod that holds the reel in place.

retrieve: One technique (and there are many) for bringing the line back in after the completion of the fly presentation; also used to impart motion to the fly during the presentation.

reverse cast: A technique in which the angler aims the forward cast away from the stream and into an open space in the trees or brush, and then turns to face the stream, completing the cast to the water.

riffles: Section of a stream where the water is completely broken but relatively shallow.

rise: The act of the fish taking an insect from the water's surface.

riseform: The type of surface disturbance created by the rise; incorrectly used as an alternative to "rise."

rock worm: A colloquial term for either caddis larva and pupa (probably because many species build their cases from small stones) or the larval stage of the crane fly (Tipulidae).

roll cast: A casting method in which the line slides across the water towards the caster and then leaves the water in a forward rolling motion, never coming back past the angler; used when there is no room behind the angler for a normal back cast.

run: A term often used to describe a particular stretch of moving water (the run below the weir pool).

running line: Another term for backing, particularly when used in reference to the backing attached to shooting head.

runoff: The high water resulting from either early summer snowmelt or recent rains.

salmon flies: Flies tied specifically for salmon fishing; also, a colloquial term for large stonefly adults, specifically the *Pteronarcys californica*.

Salmo trutta: The Latin name for brown trout.

Salvelinus fontinalis: The Latin name for brook trout (actually a char).

Salvelinus malma: The Latin name for Dolly Varden trout (actually a char).

S-cast: A casting technique in which the caster moves the rod tip from side to side at the completion of the forward cast so that the line lands on the water in a series of small curves; used to cause slack in the line to assist in getting a drag-free float when fishing dry flies.

sculpin: A bottom-feeding fish characterized by very large gills; small types are an important food form in many Western trout streams.

sedge: A common name for a caddisfly.

serpentine cast: Another term for an S-cast.

shooting: A casting technique in which the weight of a short section of line is used to pull a longer section of line along behind it; often used when there is no room for a sufficient backcast or when a very long cast must be made.

shooting basket: A small basket that can be attached to the fly fisherman's waist to hold loose line so that it can be cast by the shooting method.

shooting head: A type of fly line designed to be used with the shooting method of casting; normally only 30 feet long.

simple hatch: The emergence of only one species of aquatic insect.

single-action reel: The most common type of fly reel, which consists of a frame and a spool with a very simple drag system.

sinking line: A fly line designed so that its density is greater than that of water so that it will sink effectively.

sink rate: The speed at which a sinking fly line descends through the water. Sinking lines are available in several different sink rates.

skating spider: A dry fly with a very short hook that is wound with very large hackle so that the fly sits very high on the water. It is rapidly retrieved so that it glides, or skates, across the surface.

slack-line cast: Any one of several types of casts that end with slack line on the water.

snake cast: Another term for the S-cast or serpentine cast.

spate: High water; also, a stream is said to be "in spate" when the water is higher than normal.

spent: Exhausted or dead; usually applied to a dead insect floating on the water.

spentwing: An insect whose wings are lying out in a horizontal position, normally as a result of death.

split bamboo (cane): Another term for a bamboo, or cane, rod; derived from the way these rods are made by assembling sections of the bamboo stalk that have been split.

split shot: A small ball of lead with a slit cut into it so it can be attached to the leader; used to weight the leader and sink the fly.

steelhead trout: A sea-run rainbow trout.

stillborn flies: Insects that were malformed or otherwise unable to enter completely into the adult stage during the hatch.

stonefly: A member of the order Plecoptera.

stop cast: A casting technique in which the angler applies extra force to the forward cast and then suddenly halts the cast as the line straightens so that it bounces back towards the angler, leaving slack line on the water.

streamer: A type of artificial fly designed to imitate small minnows or baitfish.

strike indicator: A small, brightly colored piece of cork or other material attached to the leader to assist the nymph fisherman in detecting whether a fish has taken the fly.

stripping: The act of quickly retrieving line; also the act of pulling line from the reel.

taper: The shape of a fly line from end to end; e.g., forward taper, double taper. Also, a tapered leader is sometimes called a taper.

terrestrial: Of or relating to an insect whose life cycle is completed on land.

tippet: The end section of a tapered leader which is attached to the fly.

upstream: In the direction opposite to the water's flow.

waders: Another term for chest waders.

wading sandals: Sandals designed to be worn on rubber-soled hippers or waders to provide better traction through the use of felt soles.

wading shoes: Shoes that are worn over stocking-foot waders.

wading staff: A sturdy rod about as high as the angler's armpit that provides support when wading in heavy water.

weighted flies: Flies that are weighted with lead under the body so that they will sink below the surface quickly.

weight-forward line: A fly line made so that the larger diameter, heavier section has been moved towards the forward end.

wet fly: A fly that is fished below the surface, generally in imitation of an emerging insect.

wind knot: Overhand knots that occur in the leader as a result of improper casting stroke.

Zygoptera: The suborder of insects containing the dragonflies and damselflies.

METRIC EQUIVALENTS TABLE

Inches	mm	cm	Inches	cm
$1/8$	3	0.3	9	22.9
$1/4$	6	0.6	10	25.4
$3/8$	10	1.0	11	27.9
$1/2$	13	1.3	12	30.5
$5/8$	16	1.6	13	33.0
$3/4$	19	1.9	14	35.6
$7/8$	22	2.2	15	38.1
1	25	2.5	16	40.6
$1 1/4$	32	3.2	17	43.2
$1 1/2$	38	3.8	18	45.7
$1 3/4$	44	4.4	19	48.3
2	51	5.1	20	50.8
$2 1/2$	64	6.4	21	53.3
3	76	7.6	22	55.9
$3 1/2$	89	8.9	23	58.4
4	102	10.2	24	61.0
$4 1/2$	114	11.4	25	63.5
5	127	12.7	26	66.0
6	152	15.2	27	68.6
7	178	17.8	28	71.1
8	203	20.3	29	73.7

Don and Paul working on a project together.

ABOUT THE AUTHORS

PAUL FLING AND DON PUTERBAUGH have just over 100 years of combined fly-tying experience. They have taught over 1500 students to tie their own flies, have developed innovative patterns, and have tied commercially for many, many years In addition to their fly-tying instruction experience, they have run flyfishing schools in Colorado, North Carolina, and Alaska and have guided flyfishers for over 20 years on Colorado's Arkansas River. Paul now resides in South Carolina and Don lives in Colorado.

INDEX

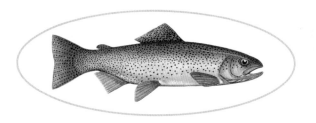